FastCourse
Microsoft®
Outlook® 2016

RICHARD DANEKE
Vanguard Information Systems

LABYRINTH
LEARNING™

Berkeley, CA

FastCourse Microsoft Outlook 2016

Copyright © 2017 by Labyrinth Learning

Labyrinth Learning
PO Box 2669
Danville, CA 94526
800.522.9746
On the web at lablearning.com

President:
Brian Favro

Product Development Manager:
Jason Favro

Development Manager:
Laura Popelka

Senior Editor:
Alexandra Mummery

Junior Editor:
Alexandria Henderson

Production Manager:
Debra Grose

Cover Design:
Mick Koller, SuperLab Design

Interior Design:
Mark Ong, Side-by-Side Studio

EBOOK ITEM: 1-59136-965-7
ISBN-13: 978-1-59136-965-3

PRINT ITEM: 1-59136-954-1
ISBN-13: 978-1-59136-954-7

Manufactured in the United States of America

GPP   10 9 8 7 6 5 4

Table of Contents

1

Getting Started with Outlook 2016

In this chapter, you will become familiar with the basics of Microsoft Outlook 2016. You will navigate the Outlook screen and customize the Quick Access toolbar, and you will observe new methods for getting help. Learning these skills early will provide you with a solid foundation to make you comfortable maneuvering around Outlook and will prepare you for learning the features introduced in later chapters.

LEARNING OBJECTIVES

- Identify the elements of Outlook
- Start the Outlook program
- Navigate the Outlook screen
- Get help on Outlook topics

CHAPTER TIMING

- Concepts/Develop Your Skills: 1 hr
- Self-Assessment: 15 mins
- Total: 1 hr 15 mins

PROJECT: GETTING TO KNOW OUTLOOK

After many years as a stay-at-home mom, Ann Hitchcock is returning to the workforce as the executive director of From Shelter to Home, a nonprofit organization that works with local assisted-living homes to help place dogs from shelters. The organization helps with the matchmaking and training of both humans and canines and also provides grants for the necessary costs to get the dogs settled in the homes. She was told during the interview that the organization uses Microsoft Outlook 2016 as its email, calendar, and contact tool. Because she has never used Outlook before, Ann wants to take a look at what the program offers and feel comfortable navigating the screen. Most important to Ann before she shows up for her first day is to know how to find help when she needs it.

Introducing Outlook 2016

Microsoft Outlook is a personal information manager that allows you to send and receive electronic mail (email), maintain an address book of all your contacts, have a place to enter personal appointments and tasks, set up meetings with others, and stay organized by reminding you of all you need to do.

What's New in Outlook 2016

Outlook 2016 is designed so you can work efficiently and quickly. The following features are new in the 2016 version. Throughout this book, you will see an icon next to the discussions of these new features:

- A new Office theme
- A help feature called "Tell me what you want to do"
- The ability to create and browse groups from the Ribbon
- The ability to press one button on the Ribbon to archive an email
- An improved file attachment process, which provides the list of recently used files
- A faster, broader Search feature
- A new Clutter folder
- An easier-to-use Attachments option
- The ability to browse and create groups from the Ribbon

Outlook Elements

Outlook is a powerful program that can do much to make your life easier. Following is a brief overview of the five major elements of Outlook:

- **Email (electronic mail):** This is the element that allows you to send and receive email messages with or without a file attached. You can save emails in separate folders to keep them organized, rather than keeping all incoming messages in the Inbox and all outgoing messages in the Sent Items folder. And with the Quick Steps feature, some of these tasks are automated for you.

- **People:** Also called Contacts, this is where you keep contact information—such as names, street addresses, phone numbers, email addresses, and web page addresses—for all of the people with whom you communicate. Contact groups can come in handy when a group of people needs to receive the same information (for example, messages sent regularly to department managers).

- **Calendar:** Calendars allow you to keep track of meetings and personal appointments, including those that recur at regular intervals. You can choose to share a calendar with others while keeping certain items private or use a calendar to remind yourself when it's time to do an activity. In addition, Outlook calendars can be used to manage room or equipment usage.

- **Tasks:** Stay on top of all of those things you need to do, people to call, things to buy, and so forth by adding them as tasks. You can assign dates, categories, and reminders to your tasks and then mark them complete as you finish them.

■ **Notes:** This component lets you store miscellaneous information that doesn't necessarily require a due date or a reminder—information that you might place on a sticky note—so you can clear your desk of clutter. For example, you may decide to store a list of account numbers or "cheat sheets" on various procedures you need to accomplish. This is the perfect, safe place to store them—instead of trying to keep track of those nasty sticky notes that always seem to disappear from around your desk.

Within each of these elements you will find items. In Outlook, an *item* is something that holds information (like a file in Microsoft Word or Excel). Depending on which Outlook element you are working in, an item may be an email message, a contact, an appointment, a task, a note, or a file.

Starting Outlook

The method you use to start Outlook is your personal preference. You can use the Start menu, a shortcut icon, or a tile. Depending on which version of Microsoft Windows you are using and how Microsoft Office was installed on your computer, your screen or procedure may differ slightly. To launch Outlook, click the Start button, navigate to Outlook 2016 in the list of apps, and click the item. When Outlook opens, you may begin working with any of its components.

The screen captures in this book show a computer with Windows 10 installed. Your screen may differ depending on your installation of Outlook and Windows.

DEVELOP YOUR SKILLS OU1-D1

Let's get started. In this exercise, you will start the Outlook program and create a basic data file without an email account.

Before You Begin: Be sure to visit the Learning Resource Center at labyrinthelab.com/lrc to retrieve the exercise files for this course before starting this exercise.

1. If necessary, start your computer.

2. Click **Start**.

3. Type Ou and then choose **Outlook 2016** from the list of programs.

4. If you have already set up Outlook on your computer, skip to **step 8**. Otherwise, go to **step 5**.

5. Click **Next** to move to the Add an Email Account screen.

6. Click in the circle to the left of **No** and then click **Next**.

7. Click in the box to the left of **Use Outlook Without an Email Account**; click **Finish**.

   ☑ Use Outlook without an email account

8. Make sure the Outlook window is maximized ☐.

Navigating the Outlook Window

The Outlook screen contains several sections with content that changes depending on which Outlook element is selected. On the left of the Outlook window is the Folder pane, in the center is the Contents pane, and on the right is the To-Do bar. You can choose whether to display or hide the To-Do bar, and you can choose what to include on it: Calendar, People, and/or Tasks. The Folder pane can be displayed, minimized, or turned off. The Navigation bar at the bottom of the Folder pane provides "peeks" into Calendar, People, or Tasks and allows you to easily switch from one element to another.

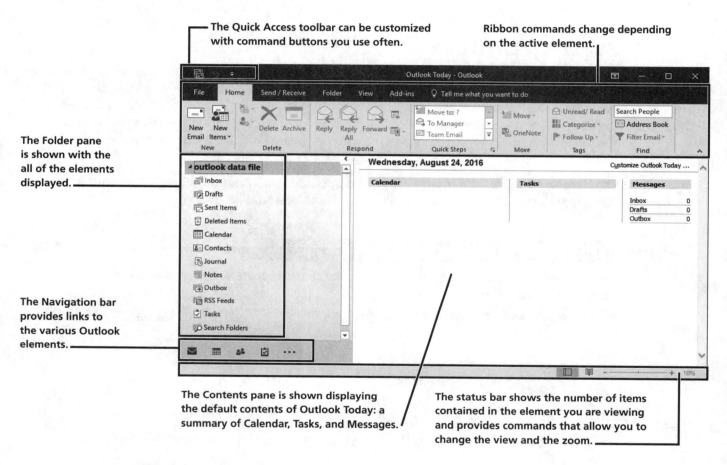

The Quick Access toolbar can be customized with command buttons you use often.

Ribbon commands change depending on the active element.

The Folder pane is shown with the all of the elements displayed.

The Navigation bar provides links to the various Outlook elements.

The Contents pane is shown displaying the default contents of Outlook Today: a summary of Calendar, Tasks, and Messages.

The status bar shows the number of items contained in the element you are viewing and provides commands that allow you to change the view and the zoom.

The Ribbon

Each Outlook window has a Ribbon with tabs that divide commands into related actions. On each tab, commands are arranged in groups, further specifying the type of action. The tabs are contextualized, meaning they are different based on which element or window you are viewing. For example, when you are in the Mail element and click the New Email button on the Outlook toolbar, the Ribbon of the resulting window displays tabs and groups of commands related to creating a new message.

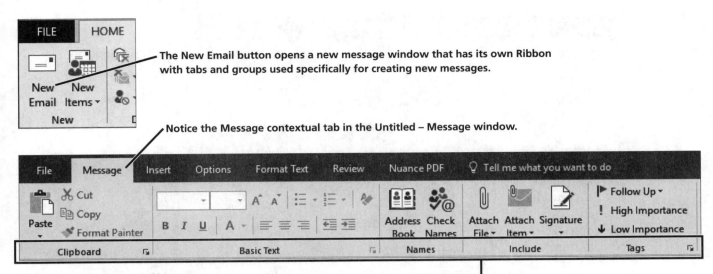

The New Email button opens a new message window that has its own Ribbon with tabs and groups used specifically for creating new messages.

Notice the Message contextual tab in the Untitled – Message window.

These are the Ribbon group names. Notice that buttons appear with some group names.

The Folder Pane

The Folder pane displays the contents of the selected Outlook element, organized in folders. When Mail is selected, the list of mail folders is displayed in the Folder pane, while the list of messages appears in the Contents pane. Folders can contain subfolders to aid in organization, and each folder has its own view that can be changed. You will know that a folder contains a subfolder when you see a white triangle next to the folder. Clicking this triangle expands and collapses the subfolders. While many aspects of Outlook can be customized, the font in the Folder pane is not one of them.

The Favorites List

One aspect of the Folder pane that can be customized is the choice of whether to display the Favorites list. When shown, this list displays at the top of the Folder pane and includes folders of your choosing that you wish to be able to access easily. The order that folders are displayed in the Favorites list is also easy to change simply by dragging the folder to a new location.

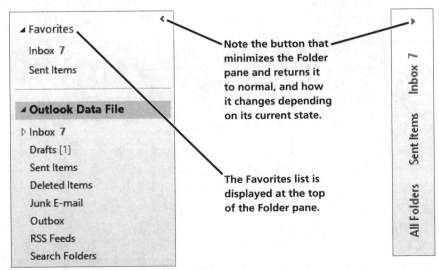

Note the button that minimizes the Folder pane and returns it to normal, and how it changes depending on its current state.

The Favorites list is displayed at the top of the Folder pane.

The Folder pane is displayed in its normal state on the left and in its minimized state on the right.

DEVELOP YOUR SKILLS OU1-D2

In this exercise, you will explore some of Outlook's Folder pane elements and the options found on the Ribbon.

1. Follow these steps to view the Folder pane features:

A Watch the New group on the Home tab as you navigate to another Outlook element, such as People. The commands change automatically.

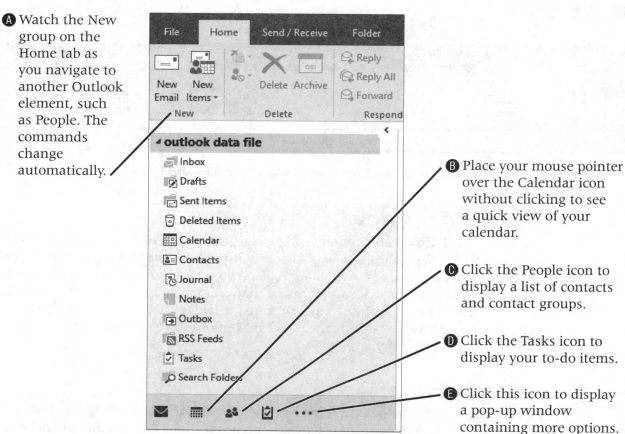

B Place your mouse pointer over the Calendar icon without clicking to see a quick view of your calendar.

C Click the People icon to display a list of contacts and contact groups.

D Click the Tasks icon to display your to-do items.

E Click this icon to display a pop-up window containing more options.

2. Click the **View** tab and then click the **Folder Pane** button in the Layout group. Click to place a checkmark next to **Favorites**, if necessary, to display the Favorites list. If you have not yet set up an account, you will see only the word *Favorites* displayed in the Folder pane.

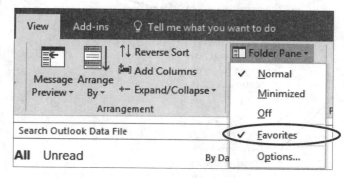

3. Click the button to minimize the Folder pane.

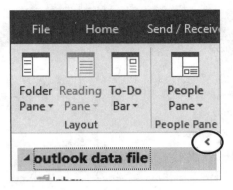

4. Click the button where the arrow now points to the right again to expand the Folder pane.

5. Click the **push pin** icon that replaces the arrow button to "pin" the Folder pane back in place.

Customizing Outlook

In Outlook, you can customize the look of all Office applications on all computers that you log in to by setting a theme.

Previously, you could choose to set the theme for all Office applications on all the computers you use, or just the theme for Outlook on the current computer. You could choose from three themes—white, light gray, and dark gray—as well as many backgrounds.

In Outlook 2016, a new *Colorful* theme has been added. The color of your Office program will now match the color of the program icons.

Personalizing the Reading Pane

The Reading pane is the section of the screen that displays the actual contents of the selected item in the Contents pane. For example, when a message in the Sent Items folder is selected, the Reading pane displays the verbiage of the message. The Reading pane can be displayed to the right of or below the Contents pane or can be hidden altogether. It can also be resized to your personal preference.

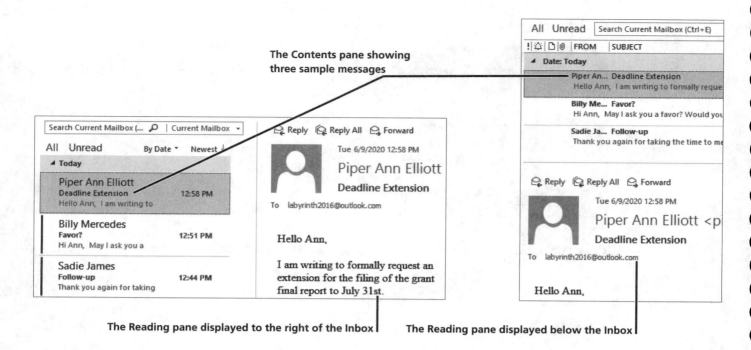

The Contents pane showing three sample messages

The Reading pane displayed to the right of the Inbox | The Reading pane displayed below the Inbox |

DEVELOP YOUR SKILLS OU1-D3

You can personalize Outlook. In this exercise, you will adjust certain Outlook features to suit your preferences.

1. Choose **File→Options** to open the Outlook Options dialog box.

2. Follow these steps to change the theme and background for Office on your computer:

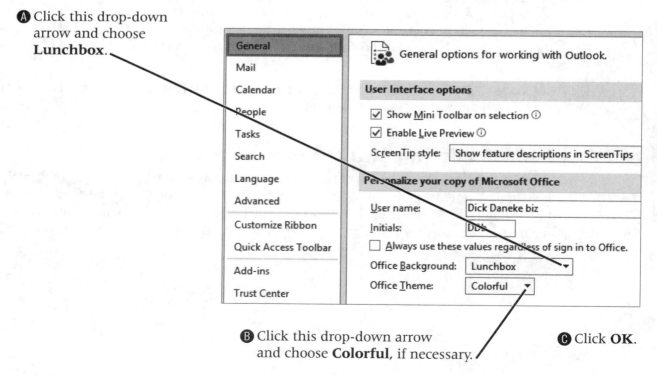

Ⓐ Click this drop-down arrow and choose **Lunchbox**.

Ⓑ Click this drop-down arrow and choose **Colorful**, if necessary.

Ⓒ Click **OK**.

3. Follow these steps to display the Reading pane below the Contents pane:

Ⓐ Choose **View→Layout→Reading Pane**. (Your panes will be blank if you don't have any messages yet.)

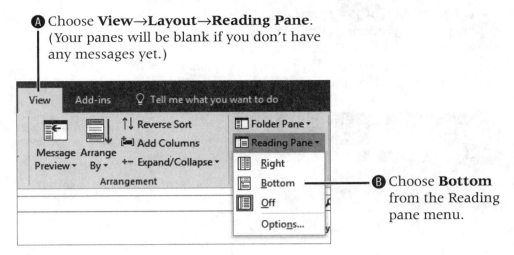

Ⓑ Choose **Bottom** from the Reading pane menu.

4. Follow these steps to resize the Reading pane:

Ⓐ Position the mouse pointer on the line between the Contents pane and Reading pane until the resize arrow appears.

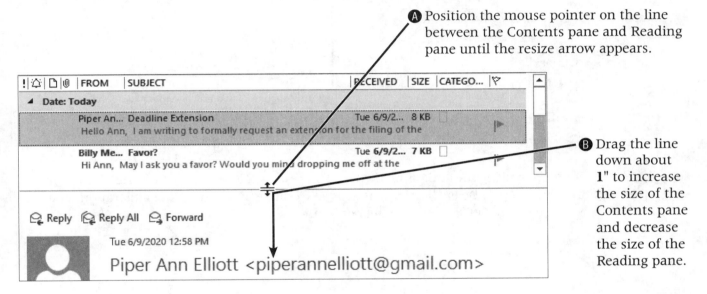

Ⓑ Drag the line down about **1"** to increase the size of the Contents pane and decrease the size of the Reading pane.

5. Choose **View→Layout→Reading Pane** and choose **Right**.
   This will move the Reading pane to the right side of the Contents area. Choose how you would like this displayed.

The Quick Access Toolbar

The Quick Access toolbar in the upper-left corner of the screen contains frequently used commands. Buttons on the Quick Access toolbar are always visible while you are in Outlook. The toolbar is customizable and operates independently from the Ribbon.

Customizing the Quick Access Toolbar

You can place the Quick Access toolbar in one of two positions: above or below the Ribbon. The default position is above the Ribbon. Clicking the More button at the right edge of the toolbar reveals a menu with some commonly used commands. From this menu, you can simply click the commands to add or remove them, open a dialog box from which to choose other commands, and change the toolbar's location.

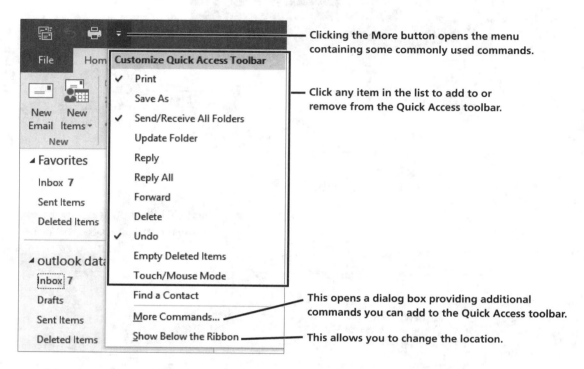

Clicking the More button opens the menu containing some commonly used commands.

Click any item in the list to add to or remove from the Quick Access toolbar.

This opens a dialog box providing additional commands you can add to the Quick Access toolbar.

This allows you to change the location.

In addition to using the options on the Quick Access toolbar menu, you can right-click any Ribbon button (the Delete button is used as an example in the following illustration) and choose the Add to Quick Access Toolbar option.

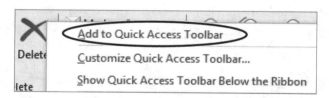

Likewise, you can right-click any button on the Quick Access toolbar and choose to remove it.

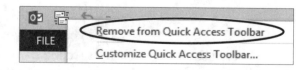

In this exercise, you will add buttons to the Quick Access toolbar, and you will find that it is more efficient to use the buttons located on the toolbar rather than those on the Ribbon.

1. Follow these steps to move the Quick Access toolbar below the Ribbon:

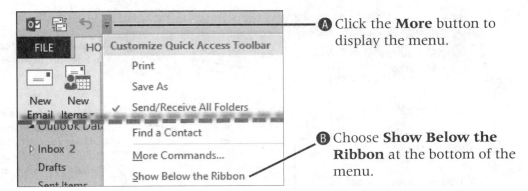

Ⓐ Click the **More** button to display the menu.

Ⓑ Choose **Show Below the Ribbon** at the bottom of the menu.

2. Click the **More** button again and then choose **Show Above the Ribbon**.

3. Click the **More** button again and then click the **Print** command to place it on the toolbar.

4. Display the **Home** tab of the Ribbon, right-click the **New Email** 🔲 button, and choose **Add to Quick Access Toolbar**.

5. Right-click the **New Email** 🔳 button on the Quick Access toolbar and choose **Remove from Quick Access Toolbar**.

Accessing Help

Microsoft Office provides a complete reference book at your fingertips. You can get the help you need for just about any Outlook topic immediately with just a few clicks. In addition to Outlook's built-in Help system, the new Tell Me What You Want to Do feature and the Office.com website offer further assistance.

 The Help and Search features in Outlook have been greatly improved with the 2016 version. A new Tell Me What You Want to Do feature has been added after the last Ribbon tab. As you will see below, it does more than simply explain Outlook features. Note, however, that in this new version, the Print icon that was previously located in the Help window and that allowed you to print hard copies of Help topics is no longer available.

Where to Get Help

You can use various methods to find the help you need. The traditional help window is still available when you press F1. All topics are linked to keywords that help identify them. For example, you can get help on printing email messages by using the keyword *print* in your search. Once you receive your results, you can leave the results window open.

Browsing for Help

Pressing F1 will open Outlook's Help window and display a list of popular help topic searches, links to training videos, suggested help topics, and a place where you can type in keywords you wish to search on. You can move backward and forward between topics or return to the Help home screen by using the Help toolbar buttons to the left of the search field.

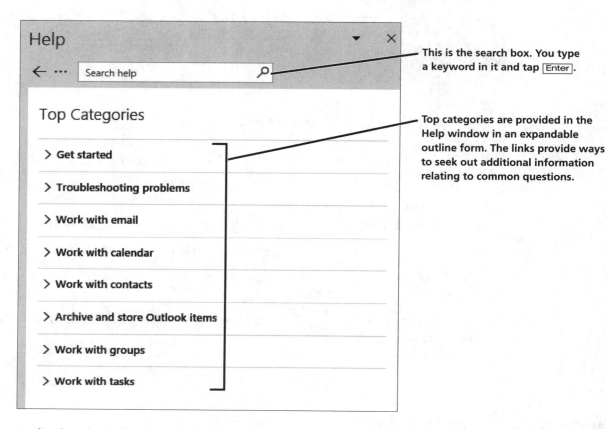

This is the search box. You type a keyword in it and tap Enter.

Top categories are provided in the Help window in an expandable outline form. The links provide ways to seek out additional information relating to common questions.

To display the Help window, press F1.

With a little research, traditional help is always close at hand. In this exercise, you will explore the help options available when you press F1.

1. Press the F1 button to open the Help pane.

2. Follow these steps to browse for help on creating a new message:

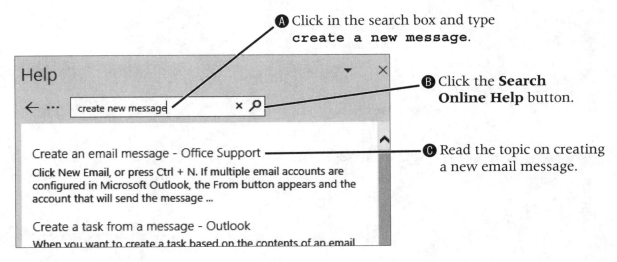

ⓐ Click in the search box and type `create a new message`.

ⓑ Click the **Search Online Help** button.

ⓒ Read the topic on creating a new email message.

3. Close the Help pane by clicking the **X** in the top-right corner of the Help pane.

Using the New Tell Me What You Want to Do Feature

The new Tell Me What You Want to Do feature describes Outlook features and delivers help topics quickly, saving you time from having to search Ribbons or dig through help topics. When you type in the Tell Me… box located to the right of the Ribbon tabs, you will start to see results as soon as you start typing. Also, instead of simply providing a help topic for you to read, this new feature sometimes even does the work for you.

DEVELOP YOUR SKILLS OU1-D6

In this exercise, you will explore the new help feature for Outlook in Office 2016.

1. Click in the **Tell Me What You Want to Do** box next to the Ribbon tabs.

2. Type **create a new message** in the box.

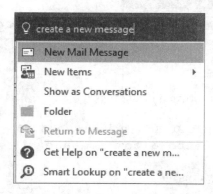

3. Click **New Mail Message**.

Outlook opens a new mail message window.

4. Close the new mail message window.

Self-Assessment

Check your knowledge of this chapter's key concepts and skills by completing the Self-Assessment. The answers to these questions can be found at the back of this book.

1. There are only two major elements in Outlook: email and the calendar.   *True   False*

2. The Quick Access toolbar can be customized with command buttons you use often.   *True   False*

3. In Outlook, items are icons found on the Ribbon.   *True   False*

4. The Reading pane can be placed to the right of or below the Contents pane.   *True   False*

5. The Reading pane shows the contents of all Outlook elements.   *True   False*

6. You can assign dates and reminders to tasks.   *True   False*

7. Contextual tabs on the Ribbon change depending on the element you are viewing.   *True   False*

8. Pressing F1 opens the Microsoft Help window.   *True   False*

9. The Folder pane displays a list of your messages.   *True   False*

10. When you open the Outlook Help window, you will see a list of popular help topic searches, training video links, and a place where you can type in keywords you wish to search on.   *True   False*

11. Which of the following is NOT a section seen in the Outlook window?
    - **A.** Folder pane
    - **B.** Navigation pane
    - **C.** Contents pane
    - **D.** To-Do bar

12. What is displayed in the Favorites list?
    - **A.** Folders of your choosing that you wish to be able to access easily
    - **B.** Your favorite people
    - **C.** Items of your choosing that you wish to access quickly
    - **D.** Items organized by contact

13. Which Outlook element should you use to remind yourself of people to call or items to buy at the store?
    - **A.** Contacts
    - **B.** Notes
    - **C.** Tasks
    - **D.** Email

14. What element are you NOT able to "peek" at from the Navigation bar?
    - **A.** Calendar
    - **B.** People
    - **C.** Tasks
    - **D.** Email

2

Working with Email

In today's personal and professional world, email has become the standard, acceptable, and easy way to communicate across your office and across the world. You can send and receive messages, documents, pictures, music, and videos. In this chapter, you will be introduced to the types of email and will learn how to set email options; how to send, read, reply to, and forward messages; and how to keep your email organized. Finally, you will search for messages without opening each folder.

LEARNING OBJECTIVES

- Set email options
- Send messages
- Handle incoming messages
- Organize messages

CHAPTER TIMING

- Concepts/Develop Your Skills: 3 hrs
- Self-Assessment: 15 mins
- Total: 3 hrs 15 mins

PROJECT: GETTING A HANDLE ON EMAIL BASICS

Now that Ann Hitchcock is familiar with the Outlook 2016 window and how to find help when she needs it, she is ready to learn to use the basic email functions in the program. She isn't too worried, as she has been using a webmail account for some time now, and she hears that there are a lot of similarities. In Ann's new job, she will be corresponding with her staff as well as staff at assisted-living homes, dog shelters, vendors, and others. Her predecessor has kept folders in a physical file cabinet for each person or organization with whom she corresponded. Ann will learn how to maintain that same organization with her electronic documents and save time when searching for a message.

Getting Started with Outlook Email

Of all the Outlook elements, email is the most widely used. It has become the standard means of communicating in the business world—and it has grown in popularity in our personal lives as well. Email is nearly as simple to use as the telephone and is a convenient way to communicate, especially when you're busy. For example, when you use the telephone, you pick up the receiver and dial a number, and then, before you actually get down to the business at hand, you usually feel the need to exchange some pleasantries. All of this takes time. However, when you send an email, you address it, type a subject, type your message, and send it on its way (still being pleasant, of course, just in less time).

Email Options

Many email options are available in Outlook. This chapter covers a couple of the most popular ones, namely adding a signature to your messages and changing the font used for new email messages.

Types of Email Accounts

You can get email accounts from various sources: your company, an Internet service provider (ISP), or, maybe more familiar to you, a webmail account such as Yahoo!® Mail, Gmail™, or Outlook.com (formerly called Hotmail). An important detail to understand is that Outlook does not create or supply you with an email account; it merely provides you with access to your accounts and a more user-friendly way to manage them.

Adding Your Email Account

Any of the email accounts just described can be set up and accessed in Outlook. You will need to know some basic information to get any of them set up, such as what type of account it is, the email address, and the password.

Email Account Settings

Settings required for your email account to work include user information, server information, and login information. Whatever you enter in the Your Name field of the User Information section is the name your recipients will see when you send them email. The email address contains a username and domain name, separated by the at (@) sign. As an example, in the email address jsmith@anycorp.com, *jsmith* is the username, and *anycorp.com* is the domain name. Companies typically decide on the username format and other configurations for the email accounts, and then a network administrator sets up Outlook and your email account. Some companies and organizations are opting to go with email solutions such as Office 365, Outlook.com, or Gmail rather than maintain their own servers and support staffing.

Outlook will try to automatically add the account with the information provided here. If additional details are required, there is a manual setup option at the bottom of the window.

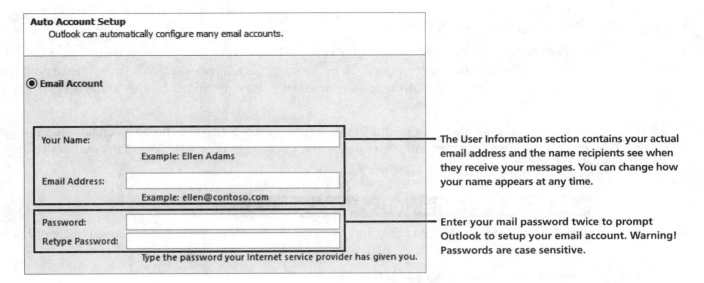

Auto Account Setup
Outlook can automatically configure many email accounts.

◉ **Email Account**

Your Name: [   ]
Example: Ellen Adams

Email Address: [   ]
Example: ellen@contoso.com

The User Information section contains your actual email address and the name recipients see when they receive your messages. You can change how your name appears at any time.

Password: [   ]
Retype Password: [   ]
Type the password your Internet service provider has given you.

Enter your mail password twice to prompt Outlook to setup your email account. Warning! Passwords are case sensitive.

Backstage View

You can find the commands to change email settings in Backstage view. This view is displayed when you click the File tab. To return to the main program, click the Back button.

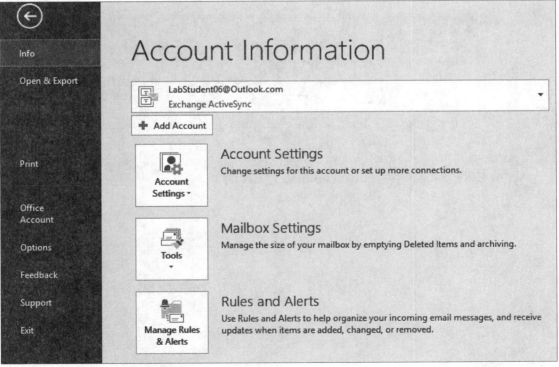

← (Back)

Info

Open & Export

Account Information

LabStudent06@Outlook.com
Exchange ActiveSync

➕ Add Account

Print

Account Settings
Account Settings ▾
Change settings for this account or set up more connections.

Office Account

Options

Mailbox Settings
Tools ▾
Manage the size of your mailbox by emptying Deleted Items and archiving.

Feedback

Support

Exit

Rules and Alerts
Manage Rules & Alerts
Use Rules and Alerts to help organize your incoming email messages, and receive updates when items are added, changed, or removed.

When you click the File tab and enter Backstage view, you will be prompted to add an email account if you do not already have one set up.

Working with Web-Based Simulations

Many of the exercises in this book are available as web-based simulations (WebSims) that require you to have an Internet connection. You can perform these exercises as WebSims or "live" using your own Outlook account.

Whenever you see the WebSim icon , you will be working as if you were actually using Microsoft Outlook; however, you will be performing the exercise on a web page. Please note that because Outlook uses your computer's system date, the dates in the figures in the book will not match the WebSims or your date.

Exercises will indicate the URLs for the WebSims. You can also use the WebSim launchpad located in your student exercise files download package to access the WebSims with a single click.

DEVELOP YOUR SKILLS OU2-D1

Outlook is used primarily for email. In this exercise, you will add an email account so you can send and receive messages.

Complete this exercise via the online WebSim.

1. In your web browser, go to **http://labyrinthelab.com/2016/websim/OU2D1**.

2. Click the **File** tab to enter Backstage view. You can use the Add Account button to open the window in step 4. If so, skip the instructions for steps 3 and 4.

3. Follow these steps to open the Account Settings dialog box:

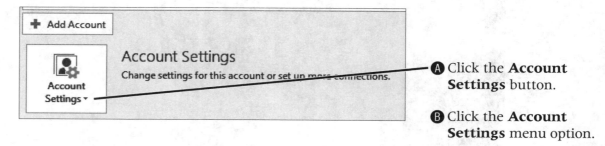

Ⓐ Click the **Account Settings** button.

Ⓑ Click the **Account Settings** menu option.

4. Click the 🖾 New… button on the Email tab.

5. Fill in the fields as indicated to create a new email account.

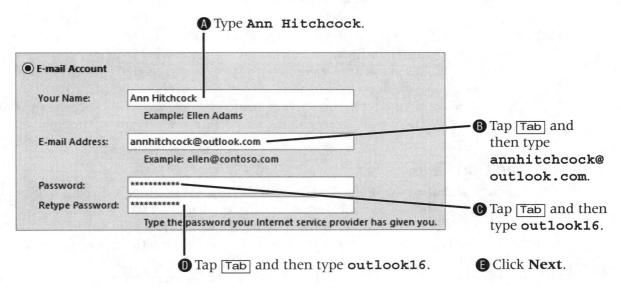

Ⓐ Type **Ann Hitchcock**.

E-mail Account

Your Name: | Ann Hitchcock

Example: Ellen Adams

E-mail Address: | annhitchcock@outlook.com

Example: ellen@contoso.com

Password: | ***********
Retype Password: | ***********

Type the password your Internet service provider has given you.

Ⓑ Tap ⌞Tab⌝ and then type **annhitchcock@ outlook.com**.

Ⓒ Tap ⌞Tab⌝ and then type **outlook16**.

Ⓓ Tap ⌞Tab⌝ and then type **outlook16**. **Ⓔ** Click **Next**.

6. If a security window pops up requesting you confirm the password, reenter the password and check the box to remember credentials.

7. Click **Finish** and then click **Close**.

Sending Messages

Most people who use Outlook are using it to send and receive email. As with other email programs, you enter addresses, type a subject in the header box, type the message, and then send it on its way. You can fill in the header boxes at the top by either clicking in them or tapping the ⌞Tab⌝ key to move through them. After an address has been entered once, Outlook remembers it. So the next time you begin typing the first few letters of it in an address box, a list of addresses beginning with those letters appears.

There are a few rules and email etiquette (also called *netiquette*) issues to point out. Some of the do's and don'ts include the following:

- Don't use spaces in an email address; it just won't work. All email addresses must follow the same format: username@domainname.com.
- Do summarize your message in the subject field. This makes it easy for your recipients to keep their messages organized. Never send an email without a subject!
- Don't type in all capital letters, as tempting as it may be. This is interpreted as YELLING. It also makes the text more difficult to read.
- Don't write anything in a message that you wouldn't be comfortable having reported on the six o'clock news.
- Do use correct capitalization and punctuation. You're not texting!
- Do type a semicolon between multiple recipients in the address boxes.

Sending to Multiple Recipients

A message can be sent to one or many recipients. When a message is sent to multiple recipients by entering addresses in the To box, everyone who receives the message will see the addresses of all other recipients. Thus, if you don't want everyone knowing to whom the message was sent, enter the addresses in the Blind Carbon Copy (Bcc) box instead. If the Bcc box is not displayed in a new message window, you can add it by using the Ribbon. You will learn more about the email Ribbon options later in this chapter. Remember to *always* use a subject line to enable you and those with whom you correspond to easily determine the topic of the email.

The Bcc Field

When all recipients are in the Bcc box, only the To and Cc fields are displayed. If some names are in the To and Carbon Copy (Cc) boxes, the Bcc recipients can see those addresses. The people in the To and Cc boxes cannot see the Bcc recipients. If you are sending a message to a large number of recipients, you may wish to include all of the email addresses in the Bcc field. This is especially helpful to those who will be viewing the message on a portable device, so that they do not have to scroll through all of the addressees. Also, if a recipient should press Reply All, the message will be sent only to the names in the To and Cc fields.

The Cc Field

A general rule for placing an address in the Cc box as opposed to the To box is that the people in the Cc box are receiving the message only for informational purposes. That is, they have no action to take and typically are not expected to reply. Some people include their own email address in either the Cc or Bcc field to have a copy of the message sent to themselves. Multiple email addresses in any of the address boxes are separated with semicolons.

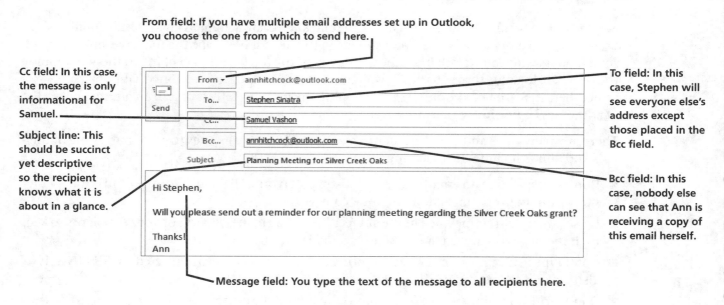

From field: If you have multiple email addresses set up in Outlook, you choose the one from which to send here.

Cc field: In this case, the message is only informational for Samuel.

Subject line: This should be succinct yet descriptive so the recipient knows what it is about in a glance.

To field: In this case, Stephen will see everyone else's address except those placed in the Bcc field.

Bcc field: In this case, nobody else can see that Ann is receiving a copy of this email herself.

Message field: You type the text of the message to all recipients here.

The Auto Complete Email List

Once you have sent a message to a recipient, Outlook "learns" the email address to make it easier for you to use again. To use these previously learned email addresses, or contacts that you already have entered into Outlook, you can easily select them from the email list that appears when you start typing an email address.

This Auto Complete list is a separate file created by Outlook and is often overlooked when changing computers. Learn more by doing a web search for *Outlook NK2 file*.

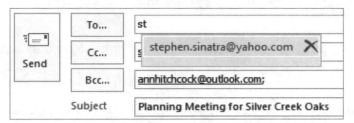

When the email list appears, you can either click an entry you wish to select or tap Tab when it is highlighted.

DEVELOP YOUR SKILLS OU2-D2

As long as you have just a few specific pieces of information, writing an email can be done quickly. In this exercise, you will fill in a form to create a new email message.

 You can complete this exercise "live" or via the online WebSim.

1. Follow the step for your situation:
   - If using the WebSim: In your web browser, go to **http://labyrinthelab.com/2016/websim/OU2D2**.
   - If using Outlook "live": Continue with step 2.
2. Choose **Home→New→New Email** 📧.
3. Follow these steps to add a Bcc field to the message window:

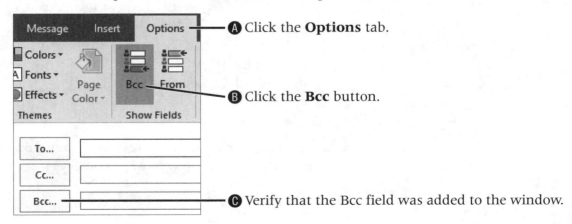

Ⓐ Click the **Options** tab.

Ⓑ Click the **Bcc** button.

Ⓒ Verify that the Bcc field was added to the window.

4. Follow these steps to create a message:

Ⓐ Click in the **To** field and type
`stephen.sinatra@yahoo.com`.

Ⓑ Click in the **Subject** line and type
`Please Contact Ahmed`.

Ⓒ Click in the message field.

5. Type the following text in the message field, tapping Enter only where indicated:

`Hi Stephen,` Enter

Enter

`Will you please call Ahmed from Eugene Field Care Facility to arrange training for his staff?` Enter

Enter

`Sincerely,` Enter

`Ann`

6. Click **Send** .

7. Choose **Home→New→New Email** .

8. Follow these steps to complete the header section of the message:

Ⓐ Begin typing `stephen`.

Ⓑ When you see the email list appear, click Stephen's email address.

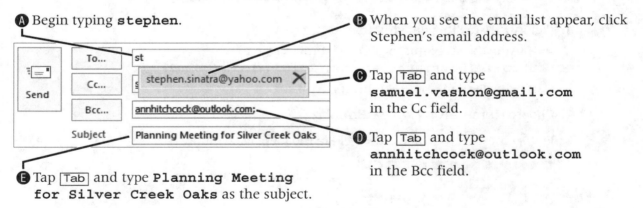

Ⓒ Tap Tab and type
`samuel.vashon@gmail.com`
in the Cc field.

Ⓓ Tap Tab and type
`annhitchcock@outlook.com`
in the Bcc field.

Ⓔ Tap Tab and type `Planning Meeting for Silver Creek Oaks` as the subject.

9. Click in the message field and type the following text:

`Hi Stephen,` Enter

Enter

`Will you please send out a reminder for our planning meeting regarding the Silver Creek Oaks partnership?` Enter

Enter

`Thanks!` Enter

`Ann`

10. Click the **Send** button.

Using Signatures to Save Time

A signature is the text you enter at the end of a message (your name, title, company, and so forth). You can create one or more signatures that Outlook will store and keep ready for you to insert at any time. You can also designate default signatures to be inserted automatically into each message you respond to or create.

When creating a new message, the Ribbon displays contextual tabs across the top. The Insert contextual tab contains buttons related to inserting something. For example, you can insert a file (which you will learn about at the end of this chapter), a picture, SmartArt, a hyperlink, or a signature. Outlook stores all of the signatures you create and lets you pick and choose which to insert in any message. The Signatures command is found in the Include group on both the Message and Insert contextual tabs.

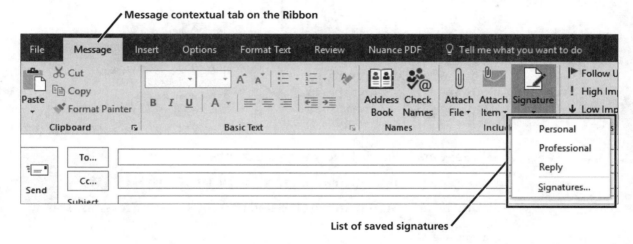

Rich formatting of your signature is available. If your signature includes any pictures or logos, ensure that the format of your message is As HTML. You can select this option in your email message window under the Format Text tab, in the Format group.

DEVELOP YOUR SKILLS OU2-D3

In this exercise, you will create new signatures that will give your emails a consistent appearance. For business purposes, a clean, professional look is expected; for personal use, you can be creative!

 You can complete this exercise "live" or via the online WebSim.

1. Follow the step for your situation:
   - If using the WebSim: In your web browser, go to
     `http://labyrinthelab.com/2016/websim/OU2D3`.
   - If using Outlook "live": Continue with step 2.
2. Choose **Home→New→New Email** ⬚.
3. Choose **Message→Include→Signature** 📝 **menu button ▼ →Signatures**.

4. Follow these steps to create a new signature:

Ⓐ Click the **New** button in the Signatures and Stationery dialog box.

Ⓑ Type **Professional** as the signature name and click **OK**.

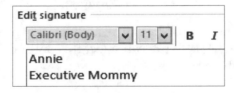

Ⓒ Click in the **Edit Signature** text box and type the text shown, tapping ⃞Enter after each line.

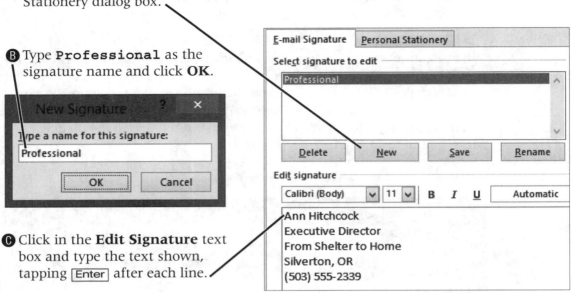

5. Click **Save** and then click **New** to create another signature.

6. Type **Personal** as the signature name and click **OK**.

7. Click in the **Edit Signature** text box and type the signature for Ann as shown:

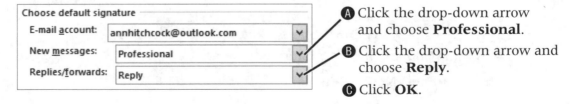

8. Click **Save** and then click **New** to create a final signature.

9. Type **Reply** as the signature name, click **OK**, and then type **Ann** as the signature text.

10. Click **Save**.

11. Follow these steps to set default signatures in the Signatures and Stationery window.

Choose default signature	
E-mail account:	annhitchcock@outlook.com ▾
New messages:	Professional ▾
Replies/forwards:	Reply ▾

Ⓐ Click the drop-down arrow and choose **Professional**.

Ⓑ Click the drop-down arrow and choose **Reply**.

Ⓒ Click **OK**.

12. Close the Untitled – Message window. If prompted, click **No** to discard the changes.

Changing and Inserting Signatures

Now that you have learned how to create a signature and how to set one up to be inserted automatically, you need to know how to insert one manually or how to change the one that was automatically inserted. Some people create multiple signatures but never set one up as a default, which is a good idea in many instances. For example, if you create a fun personal signature as a default (in our example, *Executive Mommy*) but forget about it and send a letter to the president of the company, you would probably be very embarrassed when you realized what you did. Therefore, if you set a default signature, use the one that would be most appropriate for all of your emails. In this example, you would set the Professional signature as the default.

DEVELOP YOUR SKILLS OU2-D4

In this exercise, you will quickly apply the appropriate signature to your current email message.

 You can complete this exercise "live" or via the online WebSim.

1. Follow the step for your situation:
   - If using the WebSim: In your web browser, go to **http://labyrinthelab.com/2016/websim/OU2D4**.
   - If using Outlook "live": Continue with step 2.

2. Choose **Home→New→New Email** ⬜.

3. Follow these steps to complete the header section of the message:

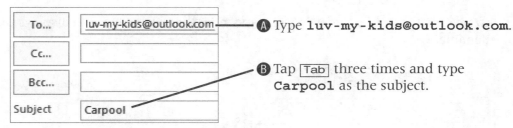

Ⓐ Type **luv-my-kids@outlook.com**.

Ⓑ Tap Tab three times and type **Carpool** as the subject.

4. Click in the message field and type this text:

   Hi Lucy, Enter
   Enter
   Could you please drive the kids' carpool for me tomorrow?

5. Choose **Message→Include→Signature** 🖉 **menu button ▼ →Personal**.

6. Click **Send** ⬜.

Attaching Files

Outlook allows you to attach other files to your messages, including a Word or Excel file, a picture, other Outlook items, and so forth. When the recipients receive the message, they can view the attachment in the Reading pane or in the associated program and also choose to save it on their computers. You will learn how to save attachments later in this chapter.

New in Outlook 2016 is a Recent Items list that appears when you use the Attach File button. This list shows you the recent files used on your computer to speed up and simplify attaching the file to your current message. Notice the small down arrow on the Attach File button that alerts you to this feature.

Both the Message tab and the Insert tab contain the Attach File command in the Include group on the Ribbon.

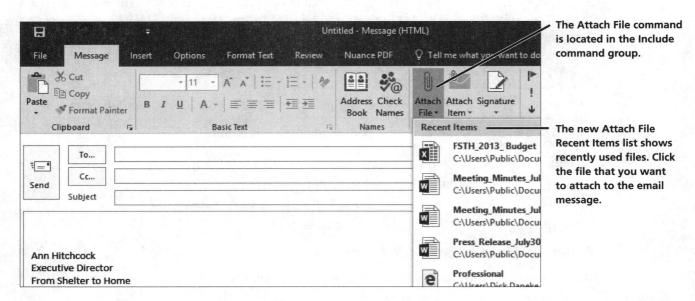

The Attach File command is located in the Include command group.

The new Attach File Recent Items list shows recently used files. Click the file that you want to attach to the email message.

After you attach a file, a new box appears under the Subject box and displays the attached filename.

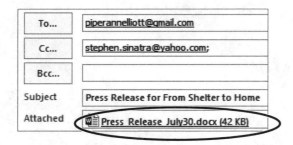

If you have included the keyword *attach* (or *attached*, *attachment*, etc.) in the email message but forget to attach the file before you choose to send, don't worry. Outlook will provide a reminder for you.

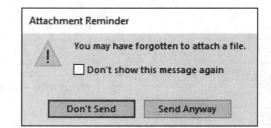

DEVELOP YOUR SKILLS OU2-D5

It has never been easier to attach the correct file. In this exercise, you will use the new fast and convenient Recent Items list feature.

 You can complete this exercise "live" or via the online WebSim.

1. Follow the step for your situation:
   - If using the WebSim: In your web browser, go to `http://labyrinthelab.com/2016/websim/OU2D5`.
   - If using Outlook "live": Continue with step 2.

2. Choose **Home→New→New Email** .

3. Address the message to `piperannelliot@gmail.com` and, in the CC field, add **Stephen Sinatra**.

4. Type `Press Release for From Shelter to Home` as the subject.

5. Click in the message field and type the message shown in the following illustration. Note that the Professional signature was added automatically.

> Hi Piper,
>
> Please find a press release attached that describes a grant that has been awarded by our organization.
>
> Sincerely,
>
> Ann Hitchcock
> Executive Director
> From Shelter to Home
> Silverton, OR
> (503) 555-2339

6. Choose **Message→Include→Attach File**.

7. Select the **Press_Release_July30** document from the Recent Items list to attach it to the email message.

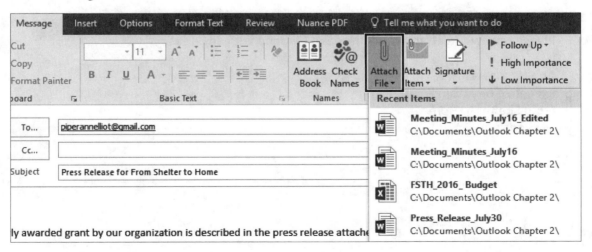

8. Send the message.

9. Click the **New Email** 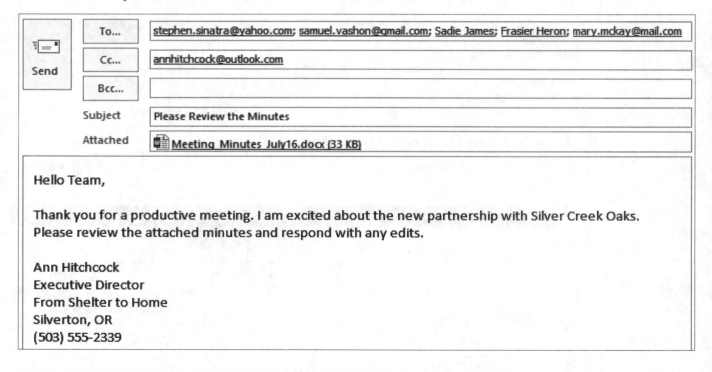 button.

10. Address the message to Sadie James and Frasier Heron. (Hint: Type the first few letters of each and choose their names from the list that appears.) If you are not using the WebSim, replace Sadie James and Frasier Heron with two of your classmates' email addresses.

11. Type **Review of Annual Budget** as the subject.

12. Type this message:

    Please review the attached budget prior to our next budget meeting.

13. Choose **Message→Include→Attach File**.

14. Select the last option in the Recent Items list, **Browse This PC**, to open the Insert File window.

15. Navigate to your **Outlook Chapter 2** folder.

16. Double-click **FSTH_2016_Budget** in the Insert File window.

17. Send the message.

18. Create and send one additional message, using the following illustration as a reference. If you are not using the WebSim, replace Sadie James and Frasier Heron in the To field with your email address and a classmate's email address.

	To...	stephen.sinatra@yahoo.com; samuel.vashon@gmail.com; Sadie James; Frasier Heron; mary.mckay@mail.com
Send	Cc...	annhitchcock@outlook.com
	Bcc...	
	Subject	Please Review the Minutes
	Attached	Meeting_Minutes_July16.docx (33 KB)

Hello Team,

Thank you for a productive meeting. I am excited about the new partnership with Silver Creek Oaks. Please review the attached minutes and respond with any edits.

Ann Hitchcock
Executive Director
From Shelter to Home
Silverton, OR
(503) 555-2339

Using Spell Check

Outlook has a spelling and grammar checker you can use to check for spelling errors in the body of a message, in an appointment, or in the Notes section of a contact. You must still proofread your messages, because the spell checker will mark a word as a possible error only if it is not in the Outlook dictionary. For example, you would probably be embarrassed if a message went out about the results of the *Broad Meeting* instead of the *Board Meeting*. You can see why proofreading is so important! The spelling and grammar checker is a shared feature across all Office programs, so if you add a new word to the dictionary in Outlook it will also then be available in a spelling check in Word, Excel, and other Office programs.

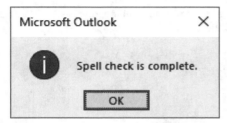

Don't believe everything you read. Once the spell check is complete, you must still proofread your message for words that may be spelled correctly but used incorrectly.

Methods to Correct Spelling Errors

A possible spelling error is indicated with a red wavy line under the word. You can fix the problems as you type, or you can wait until you have completed the message and check for errors all at once by opening the Spelling dialog box from the **Review→Proofing→ Spelling & Grammar button** or by pressing F7.

Hi Stephen,

Will you please crop in to see me before you leave for Sivler Creek Oacs? I would like to review the contract one fnial time prior to you obtaining the sgnature from Chande . This is such an important manner that I want us to get it right the first time.

Shrank you,

Notice the wavy lines indicating spelling errors. Can you find the three errors that Spell Check missed?

You can correct a mistake by clicking the right mouse button and choosing the correct word from the options menu. Alternatively, you can simply select the word and retype it.

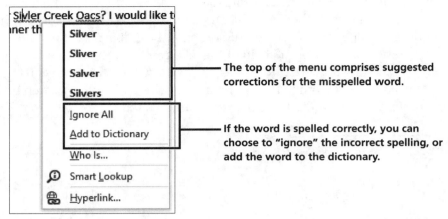

The top of the menu comprises suggested corrections for the misspelled word.

If the word is spelled correctly, you can choose to "ignore" the incorrect spelling, or add the word to the dictionary.

Notice the options that appear when you right-click Sivler.

When the Spell Checker is started from the Ribbon or by pressing F7, the upper section of the Spelling dialog box displays the entire sentence containing the error, which is highlighted in red. The lower section displays a list of possible corrections.

The Not in Dictionary box displays the sentence and highlights the possible error. You can edit the error directly if the correct suggestion is not displayed.

The Suggestions box displays possible corrections for the error.

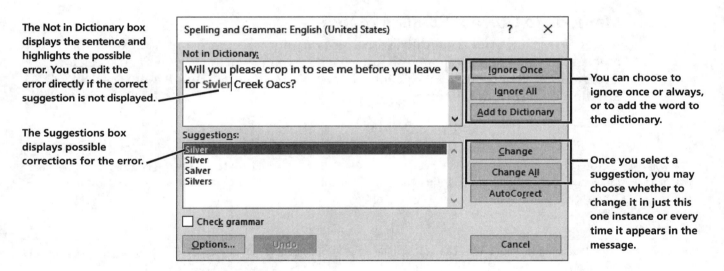

You can choose to ignore once or always, or to add the word to the dictionary.

Once you select a suggestion, you may choose whether to change it in just this one instance or every time it appears in the message.

DEVELOP YOUR SKILLS OU2-D6

In this exercise, you will see how Outlook can spot misspelled words and suggest replacements. However, remember that you still need to check your work, as it doesn't catch every error.

 You can complete this exercise "live" or via the online WebSim.

1. Follow the step for your situation:
   - If using the WebSim: In your web browser, go to `http://labyrinthelab.com/2016/websim/OU2D6`.
   - If using Outlook "live": Continue with step 2.

2. Choose **Home→New→New Email** [icon].

3. Address the message to Stephen Sinatra.

4. Type **Contract Review** as the subject.

5. Type the following message exactly as shown, including the typos; tap [Enter] as needed. Use the Professional signature that is automatically inserted.

   Hi Stephen,

   Will you please crop in to see me before you leave for Sivler Creek Oacs? I would like to review the contract one fnial time prior to your obtaining the sgnature from Chande. This is such an important manner that I want us to get it right the first time.

   Shrank you,

6. Follow these steps to correct the first highlighted spelling error:

Ⓐ Point to the misspelled word, *Sivler,* and then click the right mouse button to display the options menu.

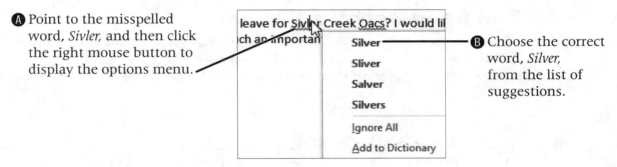

Ⓑ Choose the correct word, *Silver,* from the list of suggestions.

7. Right-click *Chande*, which is the correct spelling, and choose **Ignore All** from the options menu.

8. Choose **Review→Proofing→Spelling & Grammar** [icon].

9. Follow these steps to address the next error in the message:

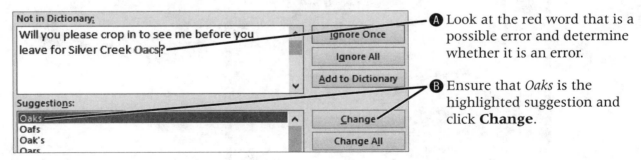

Ⓐ Look at the red word that is a possible error and determine whether it is an error.

Ⓑ Ensure that *Oaks* is the highlighted suggestion and click **Change**.

10. Click the **Change** button to accept the suggested word, *final*, for the next error.

11. Click the **Change** button to accept the suggested word, *signature*, for the next error.

12. Click **OK** in the Spelling and Grammar window. Outlook responds with a message saying that "Spell Check Is Complete," but we need to fix some words that are spelled correctly yet misused.

13. Proofread the first sentence, double-click *crop,* and type **stop**.

14. Proofread the last sentence, double-click *manner,* and type `matter`.

15. Proofread the signature, double-click *Shrank,* and type **Thank**.

16. Send the message.

Handling Incoming Messages

Outlook allows many choices of what to do with incoming messages. For example, you can read and delete, read and save, reply, forward, move to another folder, or print. If the message has a file attached to it, you can save the attachment on your hard drive or other storage device, separate from the email message.

The Send/Receive Button

Click the Send/Receive All Folders button and Outlook first sends any messages still in the Outbox and then checks the mail server for any new messages. You can check for new messages at any time by using the Send/Receive button. The Send/Receive All Folders button is located in two places. It is the first button on the Quick Access toolbar at the very top left of your program window. It is also the first button on the Send/Receive Ribbon. However, if you configure your options properly, Outlook can check for new messages on a regular basis automatically. The Send/Receive Groups window can be opened by clicking the Define Send/Receive Groups menu selection under Send/Receive Groups button in the Send & Receive group.

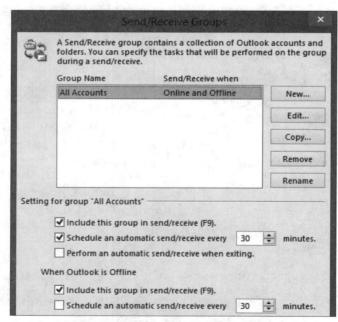

By default, Outlook is set to automatically send and receive every thirty minutes. You can change this default in the Send/Receive Groups window.

When new messages arrive, the following notifications occur (based on default settings):

- A short sound plays.
- A little icon of an unopened envelope appears in the Outlook button on the taskbar. After you open the message, the envelope disappears from the button.

DEVELOP YOUR SKILLS OU2-D7

Outlook allows you to send/receive your email in batches. In this exercise, you will determine when and how often Outlook checks for messages.

 You can complete this exercise "live" or via the online WebSim.

1. Follow the step for your situation:
   - If using the WebSim: In your web browser, go to **http://labyrinthelab.com/2016/websim/OU2D7**.
   - If using Outlook "live": Continue with step 2.

2. Choose **Send/Receive→Send & Receive→Send/Receive All Folders** .

3. Choose **Send/Receive→Send/Receive Groups→Define Send/Receive Groups**.

4. Follow these steps to change the send/receive settings in the bottom of the options window:

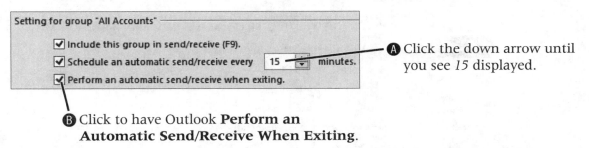

Ⓐ Click the down arrow until you see *15* displayed.

Ⓑ Click to have Outlook **Perform an Automatic Send/Receive When Exiting**.

5. Click **Close** in the Send/Receive window and **OK** in the Send/Receive Groups window.

Reading Messages

A new message is displayed first in the Inbox. By default, the message is indicated as new with bold, blue type. To mark a message as unread, move your mouse pointer over the blue bar and click to change the status of the message.

When you place your mouse pointer over a message, it becomes highlighted and icons appear that will assist you in working with the message. For instance, an attachment is indicated with a small paperclip. You can read the contents of the message in the Reading pane, or you can double-click the message to open it in its own window. The latter method is helpful if the message is unusually long, because the larger window may enable you to view all of the message without having to scroll down.

The mail view allows you to easily preview your messages before you open them. You will also see message list commands that appear when you move your mouse pointer over a message.

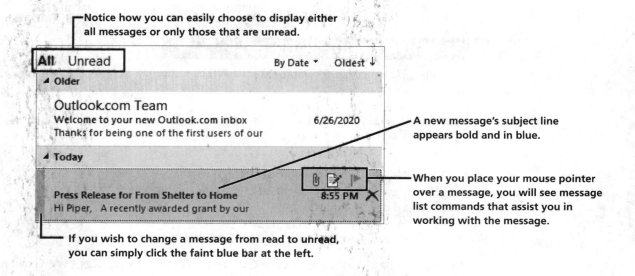

Notice how you can easily choose to display either all messages or only those that are unread.

A new message's subject line appears bold and in blue.

When you place your mouse pointer over a message, you will see message list commands that assist you in working with the message.

If you wish to change a message from read to unread, you can simply click the faint blue bar at the left.

You can also mark a message as unread from the Message window.

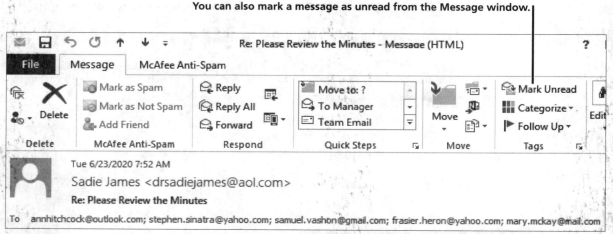

Notice that when you double-click a message in the Inbox, it opens in its own window and has its own Ribbon. In the preceding example, McAfee virus protection has been installed on this computer, so a contextual tab is available to access the McAfee tools.

Saving Attachments

When you receive a message with an attachment, you will notice the name of the file in the message box directly above the body of an actual email message. Some file types, such as Word or Excel files, open automatically when you double-click the attachment. Other files, such as graphics files, display an Opening Mail Attachment dialog box with options to open or save. You can also right-click an attachment to display a menu with such options as Open, Save As, and Quick Print. A word of caution is important here as viruses are often passed through email messages and their attachments, especially those with an extension of .exe. Be very mindful of the type of file and who it is from before you open it.

When you right-click a message attachment, you will see an options menu from which you can choose to save the attachment.

When you attempt to open some types of attachments, you will see the Opening Mail Attachment dialog box to warn you of possible dangers.

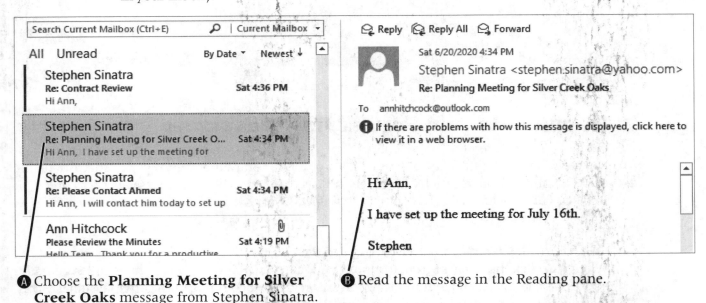

Opening Mail Attachment

❓ You should only open attachments from a trustworthy source.

Attachment: FSTH_Logo.bmp from Inbox - annhitchcock@outlook.com - Outlook

Would you like to open the file or save it to your computer?

[Open]   [Save]   [Cancel]

☑ Always ask before opening this type of file

✉ Message   📄 Meet...

Hello Team,

Thank you for a produ
attached minutes and

| Preview |
| Open |
| Quick Print |
| Save As |
| Save All Attachments... |
| Remove Attachment |

DEVELOP YOUR SKILLS OU2-D8

When you receive emails containing attached files, you have options. In this exercise, you will open such a file and then save the attachment.

You can complete this exercise "live" or via the online WebSim.

1. Follow the step for your situation:
   - If using the WebSim: In your web browser, go to
     `http://labyrinthelab.com/2016/websim/OU2D8`.
   - If using Outlook "live": Continue with step 2.

2. Follow these steps to read a message (if you are not using the WebSim, choose any message in your Inbox):

Search Current Mailbox (Ctrl+E) 🔍 | Current Mailbox ▾

All   Unread   By Date ▾   Newest ↓

Stephen Sinatra
Re: Contract Review   Sat 4:36 PM
Hi Ann,

Stephen Sinatra
Re: Planning Meeting for Silver Creek O...   Sat 4:34 PM
Hi Ann, I have set up the meeting for

Stephen Sinatra
Re: Please Contact Ahmed   Sat 4:34 PM
Hi Ann, I will contact him today to set up

Ann Hitchcock   📎
Please Review the Minutes   Sat 4:19 PM
Hello Team, Thank you for a productive

🔁 Reply   🔁 Reply All   ➡ Forward

Sat 6/20/2020 4:34 PM
Stephen Sinatra <stephen.sinatra@yahoo.com>
Re: Planning Meeting for Silver Creek Oaks

To   annhitchcock@outlook.com

ℹ If there are problems with how this message is displayed, click here to view it in a web browser.

Hi Ann,

I have set up the meeting for July 16th.

Stephen

Ⓐ Choose the **Planning Meeting for Silver Creek Oaks** message from Stephen Sinatra.

Ⓑ Read the message in the Reading pane.

3. Follow these steps to save an attachment (if you are not using the WebSim, choose any message in your Inbox with an attachment):

Ⓐ Choose the **Please Review the Minutes** message from Sadie James.

Ⓑ Right-click the attached file.

Ⓒ Choose **Save As**.

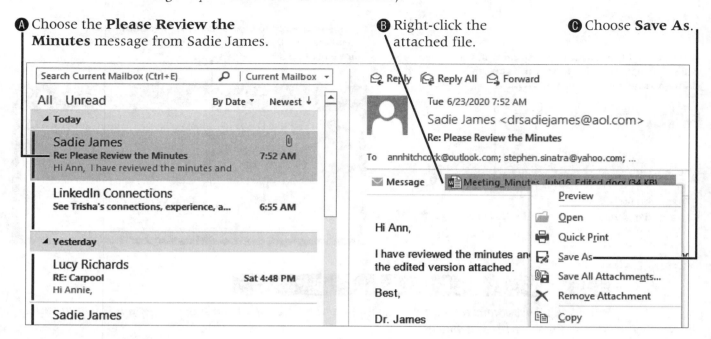

Ⓓ Navigate to your file storage location.

Ⓔ Click **Save**.

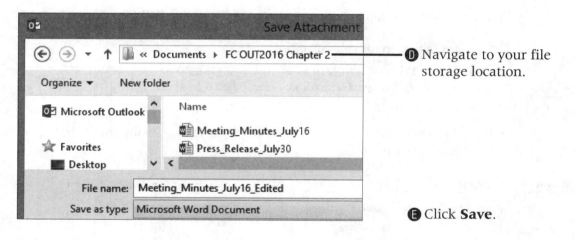

Replying to and Forwarding Messages

Outlook makes it easy for you to reply to a message or to share it with others by forwarding it. You may change the subject when replying to or forwarding a message, if you wish. Outlook offers a Show as Conversations option on the View tab that will group messages based on Subject. This provides a convenient way to follow the exchange of emails on a specific topic.

Reply or Reply All

When you click the Reply button, Outlook opens a new window and places the sender's email address in the To box and automatically inserts *Re:* at the beginning of the original subject. This feature is extremely helpful because it takes the worry out of making a mistake retyping the sender's email address. Outlook also includes a copy of the sender's original message in the message box so it will be easy for the sender to see exactly what you are replying to. If you want to send your reply to everyone who originally received the message, you can use the Reply All button instead of the Reply button. Use the Reply All feature cautiously. If everyone on the original message really doesn't need to see your reply, don't use it! Most people get plenty of email, so don't burden them with messages they do not need.

Forwarding a Message

You may receive a message that you would like to share with others. You can do this with the Forward command. As with replying, Outlook opens a new window, but this time it leaves the To box empty so you can enter the email address to which you would like to forward the message. When you forward a message, Outlook inserts *Fw:* in front of the original subject. This lets the recipients know without opening the message that it has been forwarded through you from someone else. And remember, when someone forwards you a file, you don't really know where it came from. Always be careful when opening messages and attachments.

Note the options on the Message window Ribbon that allow you to reply to or forward messages.

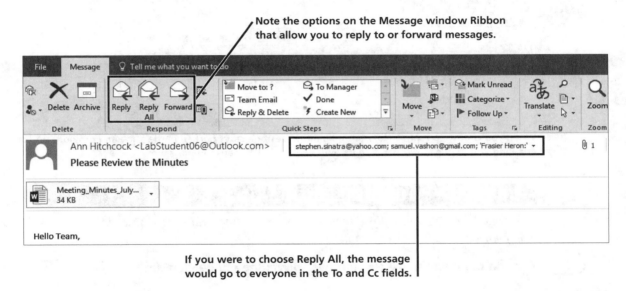

If you were to choose Reply All, the message would go to everyone in the To and Cc fields.

Inline Replies

Outlook allows you to reply to and forward messages from within the Reading pane. These are called *inline replies*.

When composing a message in the Reading pane, you have two additional choices: You can quickly discard the message or pop your reply out of the Reading pane into a separate window.

When viewing a message in the Reading pane, you can choose to quickly reply or forward it inline.

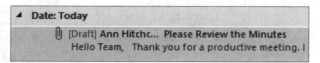

Once you choose to reply to or forward a message, Outlook places *[Draft]* in front of the sender's name of the email in the Contents pane.

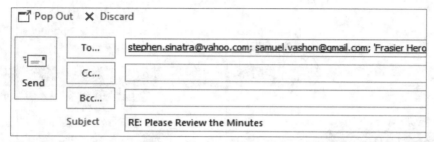

When you choose to reply or forward inline, the message stays docked in the pane and provides buttons enabling you to Pop Out (open it in its own window) or Discard the message.

DEVELOP YOUR SKILLS OU2-D9

In this exercise, you will reply to the sender of an existing email message and forward another message, along with your commentary on it, to someone else.

 You can complete this exercise "live" or via the online WebSim.

1. Follow the step for your situation:
   - If using the WebSim: In your web browser, go to `http://labyrinthelab.com/2016/websim/OU2D9`.
   - If using Outlook "live": Continue with step 2.

2. Follow these steps to reply to a message; if not using the WebSim, choose another email in your Inbox:

Ⓐ Click the **Please Review the Minutes** reply from Sadie James.   Ⓑ Click **Reply**.

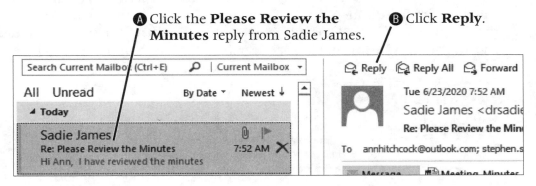

3. Type this message: `Thank you for catching the omission.`

4. Send the message.

5. Follow these steps to forward a message; if not using the WebSim, select any email in your Inbox:

Ⓐ Click the **Review of Annual Budget** reply from Sadie James.   Ⓑ Click **Forward**.

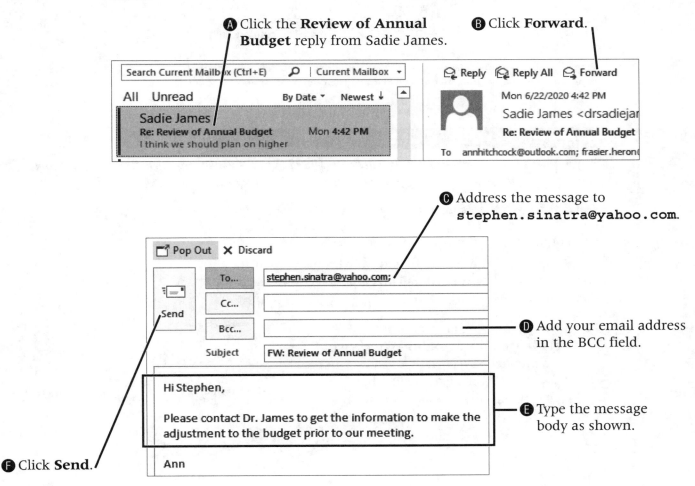

Ⓒ Address the message to `stephen.sinatra@yahoo.com`.

Ⓓ Add your email address in the BCC field.

Ⓔ Type the message body as shown.

Ⓕ Click **Send**.

Flagging Messages

Many times you will read a message and know that you need to take further action on it. You can choose to flag the message right from the Follow Up button on the Ribbon or by clicking in the Follow Up column of your current message in the folder. These flagged messages will be added to your To-Do list, and you can search for them in your Inbox as well.

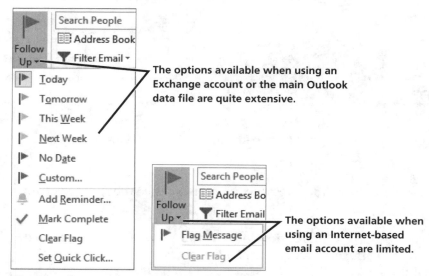

The options available when using an Exchange account or the main Outlook data file are quite extensive.

The options available when using an Internet-based email account are limited.

When you choose Home→Tags→Follow Up, the resulting menu will look different depending on whether you are using an Exchange account or an Internet account such as Outlook.com.

DEVELOP YOUR SKILLS OU2-D10

As you start to receive more emails, you decide you need to find a way to organize them. In this exercise, you will quickly flag a message in your email list to indicate that further action is required.

 You can complete this exercise "live" or via the online WebSim.

1. Follow the step for your situation:
   - If using the WebSim: In your web browser, go to
     `http://labyrinthelab.com/2016/websim/OU2D10`.
   - If using Outlook "live": Continue with step 2.

2. Move your mouse pointer over the **Re: Please Contact Ahmed** message from Stephen and click the red flag when it appears. If you are not using the WebSim, flag any message in your Inbox.

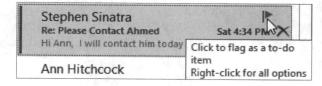

Printing Messages

You can print a message just as you print any other document. From Backstage view, you can preview the selected message and choose print options. The default style to print messages is called Memo style. It prints your name, the message header information (such as subject and date), and the message content. The Table style prints the list of items being displayed in the Contents window, such as the list of emails in the Inbox.

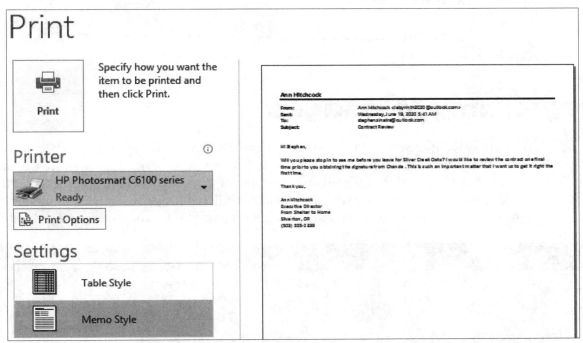

In Backstage view, you can select a printer, choose whether to print in Table or Memo style, and issue the print command. To the right of these options, you can also see a preview of what the message will look like printed.

To print an attachment, you first open the attachment and then print from its associated program. For example, Microsoft Excel opens for an Excel spreadsheet attachment, Microsoft Word opens for a standard Word document, Adobe Acrobat opens for a PDF file attachment, and so forth. Or, you can also choose to Quick Print to your default printer if you right-click the attachment. Outlook then opens the program used to create the attachment and automatically prints the file.

DEVELOP YOUR SKILLS OU2-D11

When working in an office, you often need to print an email for sharing or archiving purposes. In this exercise, you will print a message and its attachment.

 You can complete this exercise "live" or via the online WebSim.

1. Follow the step for your situation:
   - If using the WebSim: In your web browser, go to **http://labyrinthelab.com/2016/websim/OU2D11**.
   - If using Outlook "live": Continue with step 2.

2. Select any email message with an attachment.

3. Choose **File→Print** and then choose **Print Options** to display the Print dialog box.

4. Follow these steps to print the message with its attachment:

Ⓐ Click to place a checkmark in the **Print Attached Files** box.

Ⓑ Click **Print**.

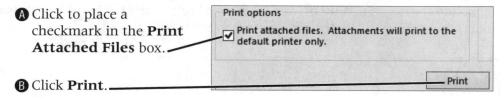

Organizing Messages

You may want to keep some messages you send or receive for future reference. Leaving all incoming messages in the Inbox and outgoing messages in the Sent Items folder can become overwhelming as the number of messages grows. Typically, you will have messages that somehow relate to one another. For example, you may send and receive messages for meetings or special projects. An easy way to keep the messages organized is to store them in separate folders.

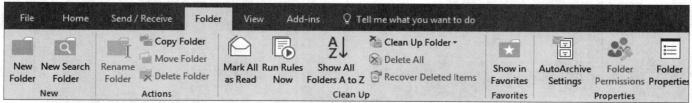

The Folder tab of the Ribbon provides options to help manage your folders.

Creating Folders

The folder structure you decide upon should be the one that works best for you. For example, maybe you work on multiple projects. In that case, creating folders for each project name and saving messages related to each project can help keep you organized. In the illustration displayed, you can see that Ann has chosen to create folders for the facilities with which she is working. You can use the Folder tab on the Ribbon to create a new folder, or simply right-click an existing folder and choose New Folder from the menu to create a subfolder. New folders are placed in alphabetical order among the other folders.

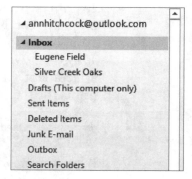

Adding Folders to Favorites

You can add a list called Favorites to the top of the Folder pane. You get to choose which folders Outlook displays here, based on how you use the program. The initial order in which the folders are displayed is based on the order in which they were added to the list. However, you can drag the folders to place them in any order you prefer. You can also add or delete folders from your Favorites at any time.

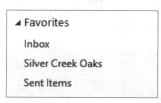

Ann has chosen to include three folders in her Favorites.

A New Folder Named Clutter

A new folder named Clutter has been added in Outlook 2016. Clutter helps you manage the low-priority messages that can quickly fill up and clutter your Inbox. Outlook analyzes your emails and, based on your past actions, determines which messages you are most likely to ignore. You can accelerate this learning process by moving messages from your Inbox into the new Clutter folder.

DEVELOP YOUR SKILLS OU2-D12

Saved emails can be placed into folders, just as paper documents are organized into folders in filing cabinets. In this exercise, you start organizing your saved messages by creating your own folders in Outlook.

 You can complete this exercise "live" or via the online WebSim.

1. Follow the step for your situation:
   - If using the WebSim: In your web browser, go to
     http://labyrinthelab.com/2016/websim/OU2D12.
   - If using Outlook "live": Continue with step 2.

2. Right-click the **Inbox** folder and choose **New Folder** from the menu.

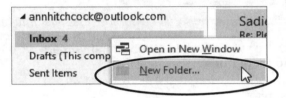

3. Type **Silver Creek Oaks** and tap Enter.

4. Right-click the **Inbox** folder again and choose **New Folder**.

5. Type **Eugene Field** and tap Enter.

6. Follow these steps to add a folder to your Favorites:

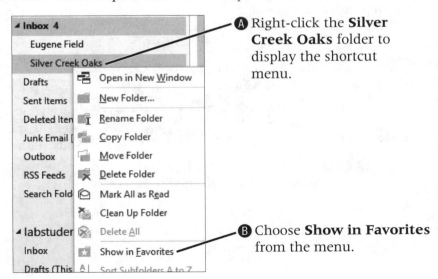

Ⓐ Right-click the **Silver Creek Oaks** folder to display the shortcut menu.

Ⓑ Choose **Show in Favorites** from the menu.

7. Click in the new **Silver Creek Oaks** folder within Favorites.

Moving and Copying a Message to a Folder

Once you have folders created, you can move new incoming or outgoing messages into them. Two methods for moving a message to a folder are via a Ribbon command or by using drag and drop.

You can copy a message and place it in a folder by holding down the Ctrl key when dragging it onto a folder. Or, you can use the Copy to Folder command on the drop-down menu of the Move button in the Move group on the Ribbon.

Moving or Copying a Group of Messages

At times messages will fly back and forth: incoming, replying, forwarding, sending, and so forth. You may not take the time with each and every message to immediately move it into a folder. No worry; you can select multiple messages and move them all at the same time from any folder into another one. To select multiple messages, hold down Ctrl and click individual messages in the list. Or, if you want to select the complete list or adjacent messages in a list, you can select the first message you want, hold down Shift, and then click the last one you want. The entire list is then highlighted and ready to move, copy, or even delete.

DEVELOP YOUR SKILLS OU2-D13

There are several ways to file your emails. In this exercise, you will move messages into an existing folder.

 You can complete this exercise "live" or via the online WebSim. If you are working "live," use any email in your Inbox that you no longer need.

1. Follow the step for your situation:
    - If using the WebSim: In your web browser, go to **http://labyrinthelab.com/2016/websim/OU2D13**.
    - If using Outlook "live": Continue with step 2.

2. Click to display the **Inbox**.

3. Follow these steps to move a message:

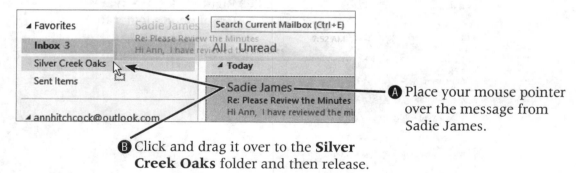

Ⓐ Place your mouse pointer over the message from Sadie James.

Ⓑ Click and drag it over to the **Silver Creek Oaks** folder and then release.

4. Follow these steps to select three messages to move to a folder:

 **(A)** Click **Sent Items**.

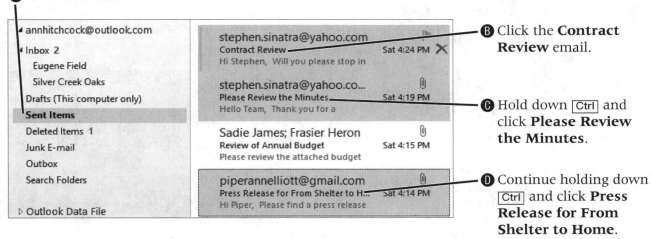

(B) Click the **Contract Review** email.

(C) Hold down [Ctrl] and click **Please Review the Minutes**.

(D) Continue holding down [Ctrl] and click **Press Release for From Shelter to Home**.

5. Choose **Home→Move→Move** 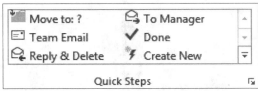 **→Other Folder**.

6. Choose **Silver Creek Oaks** from the menu.

Quick Steps

Microsoft Outlook has a fantastic, time-saving feature called Quick Steps. There are built-in quick steps that can be customized—or you can create your own. Quick Steps help by automating repetitive tasks. For example, suppose a message arrives that you would like to forward to your manager. With one click of the button, the task can be completed. The first time you use each Quick Step, you will be prompted for relevant information to customize this Quick Step in the future. From then on, it takes only one click to activate the command. What a time-saver!

Move to: ?	To Manager
Team Email	Done
Reply & Delete	Create New
Quick Steps	

Quick Steps can be found on the Home tab. By default, five are created for you.

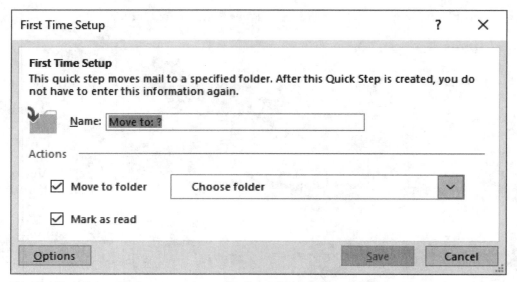

The First Time Setup window prompts you for the action steps for each message.

Rules

Rules are not Quick Steps. They are shown under the Rules button in the Move group of the Home tab. Rules can be set up in Outlook to automate certain tasks. Quick Steps are rules that you choose to apply to situations in Outlook. Rules are automatically applied. For instance, you can have messages that meet certain criteria automatically move into a specific folder. Or, you can choose for Outlook to play a specific sound when you receive a message from a particular person. The Create Rule window is prefilled with options based on the open message.

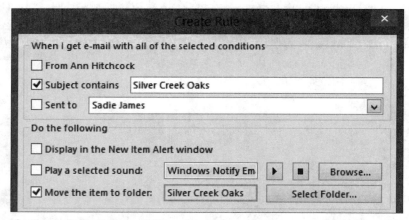

The Create Rule window allows you to set up rules to automate specific tasks in Outlook.

In this exercise, you will create a Quick Step rule that will speed up the routine handling of regular messages.

 You can complete this exercise "live" or via the online WebSim.

1. Follow the step for your situation:
   - If using the WebSim: In your web browser, go to **http://labyrinthelab.com/2016/websim/OU2D14**.
   - If using Outlook "live": Continue with step 2.

2. Click the **Inbox** in the **Folder** pane.

3. Choose **Home→Quick Steps→Move To** .

4. Follow these steps to set up the Quick Step:

Ⓐ Type **Move to SCO**.

Ⓑ Click the drop-down arrow and choose **Silver Creek Oaks**.

Ⓒ Click **Save**.

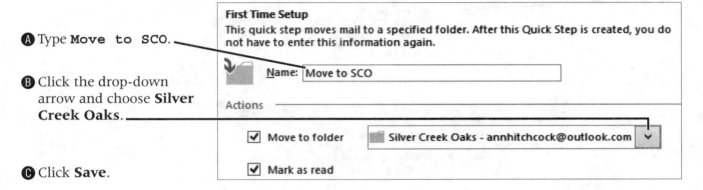

First Time Setup
This quick step moves mail to a specified folder. After this Quick Step is created, you do not have to enter this information again.

Name: Move to SCO

Actions

☑ Move to folder Silver Creek Oaks - annhitchcock@outlook.com

☑ Mark as read

5. Follow these steps to use the new Quick Step:

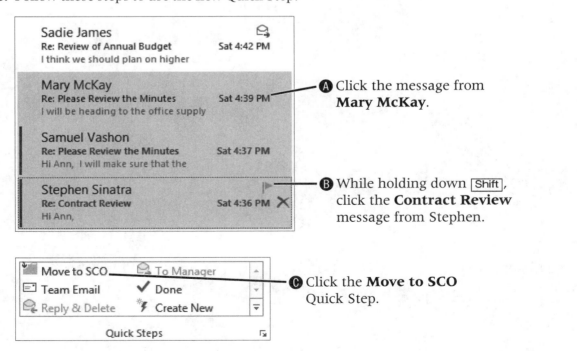

Sadie James
Re: Review of Annual Budget   Sat 4:42 PM
I think we should plan on higher

Mary McKay
Re: Please Review the Minutes   Sat 4:39 PM
I will be heading to the office supply

Ⓐ Click the message from **Mary McKay**.

Samuel Vashon
Re: Please Review the Minutes   Sat 4:37 PM
Hi Ann, I will make sure that the

Stephen Sinatra
Re: Contract Review   Sat 4:36 PM
Hi Ann,

Ⓑ While holding down [Shift], click the **Contract Review** message from Stephen.

Move to SCO   To Manager
Team Email   ✔ Done
Reply & Delete   Create New

Quick Steps

Ⓒ Click the **Move to SCO** Quick Step.

6. Choose **Home→Move→Rules menu button ▼ →Create Rule**.

7. Follow these steps to create the new rule:

Ⓐ Click the **Subject Contains** checkbox.

Ⓑ Tap [Tab] and type **Silver Creek Oaks**.

Ⓒ Click the **Move the Item to Folder** checkbox.

Ⓓ Click **Silver Creek Oaks**.

Ⓔ Click **OK**.

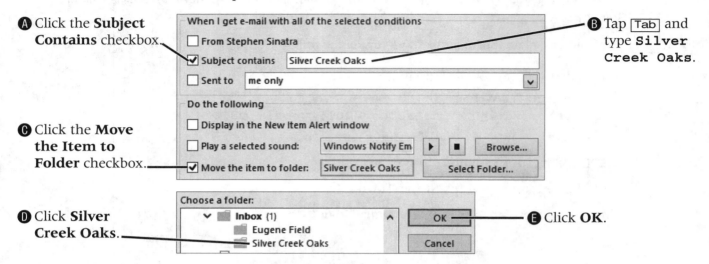

8. Click **OK** in the Create Rule window.

9. Click in the **Run This Rule Now...** checkbox and then click **OK**.

Sorting Messages in a Folder

Email is such a popular method of communicating today that the number of messages in the Inbox and Sent Items boxes can quickly add up. And, even if you have created folders to store related messages, when you're looking for that one special message you need to refer to, finding it quickly can sometimes pose a problem. Outlook allows you to easily sort your messages in the selected folder. By default, Outlook sorts by date, from newest to oldest. To locate a message you need, you can change the criteria by which messages are sorted.

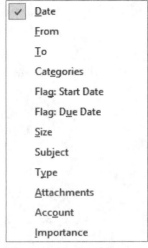

There are 12 criteria by which you can sort your messages.

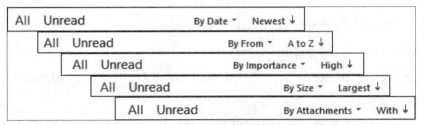

Notice that as you change the criteria by which you sort your messages, the order listed changes as well.

Searching for a Message

If you were not able to easily find a message by sorting the messages in a folder, you may wish to search for it instead. Outlook's search feature works much like most others—that is, by typing a keyword contained in a message. Initially, the search is performed on the location showing in the right side of the search box. If it's not found there, you can switch the search location with options provided in the right side box of the Search window.

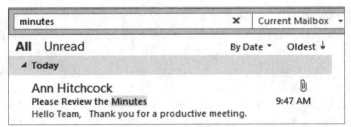

To find the message she sent with the meeting minutes attached, Ann searched using the keyword *minutes*. Outlook highlights the keyword when it displays the results.

Outlook 2016 email search has been updated and enhanced to make finding the right messages faster. Now you can search seamlessly across your email folders and remote mailboxes. Much like Internet searching, search suggestions will appear to assist in completing your search.

You have a computer assistant! The Search window can assist you in locating Outlook items. In this exercise, you will search for messages from a specific person and then for messages containing a particular name.

 You can complete this exercise "live" or via the online WebSim.

1. Follow the step for your situation:
   - If using the WebSim: In your web browser, go to
     `http://labyrinthelab.com/2016/websim/OU2D15`.
   - If using Outlook "live": Continue with step 2.

2. Click the **Silver Creek Oaks** folder in the Folder list.

3. Click the **Sent Items** folder in the Folder pane.

4. Click in the **Search Sent Items** box at the top of the Inbox and type **ahmed**.

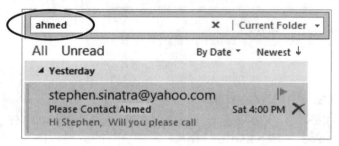

5. Click the **Close** ✕ button to the right of *ahmed* to close the search.

Deleting Messages

When you delete a message, it is sent to the Deleted Items folder. It's important to note that the message is still in your Outlook files until you empty this folder. The nice thing about this is that if you delete a message by mistake, until the Deleted Items folder is emptied, you can move the message back into any other Outlook folder. If you are using Outlook in a corporate setting, your systems administrator probably has set up an automated system whereby your Deleted Items folder is emptied on a regular basis. You can empty the folder manually at any time by right-clicking the Deleted Items folder and choosing Empty Folder. Just as with moving a group of messages at the same time, you can use the same procedure for selecting a group of messages to delete. In Outlook, you can delete a message with one click of the ✕ in the list of messages in your current folder. You can also delete the selected message using the Ribbon.

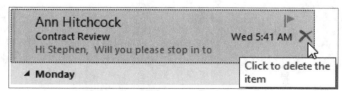

When you move your mouse pointer over a message, a red ✕ appears on the right side; clicking it deletes the message and moves it to the Deleted Items folder.

Most messages do not need to be saved forever. In this exercise, you will delete a message and then empty the Deleted Items folder.

 You can complete this exercise "live" or via the online WebSim.

1. Follow the step for your situation:
   - If using the WebSim: In your web browser, go to **http://labyrinthelab.com/2016/websim/OU2D16**.
   - If using Outlook "live": Continue with step 2.

2. Click **Sent Items** in the Folder pane.

3. Click the first message in the list that will be okay to delete.

4. Hold down the $\boxed{\text{Shift}}$ key and click the last message you can see in the list.

5. Release $\boxed{\text{Shift}}$ and tap $\boxed{\text{Delete}}$ to move the messages to the Deleted Items folder.

6. If you need to keep the emails, press $\boxed{\text{Ctrl}}$ + $\boxed{\text{Z}}$ to move the emails back to their original folder.

7. Right-click **Deleted Items** in the Folder pane and choose **Empty Folder** from the menu.

8. Choose **Yes** in the message box that displays.

Archiving Messages

All items in Outlook are stored in a special Outlook data file. As you accumulate more and more messages and other items such as calendars, the data file becomes especially large, which can ultimately slow Outlook's performance. You can free up space by creating a separate Archive folder. There may be messages that you do not need to keep in current folders but that you don't want to delete immediately. For example, you may have many messages related to an old project. It's possible that, in the future, you may need to refer to some information contained in those messages. Archive folders are available for the other Outlook components also. So, you could keep copies of your old calendars, for example.

You create subfolders in the Archive folder exactly the same way you create them in any other folder. You can move messages into the subfolders in Archive by using the same methods as for other folders. Create your own archive subfolders in the Archive Folders Inbox and move messages into them accordingly.

New in Outlook 2016 is an Archive button added to the Delete group on the Home tab. Highlight one or more messages and click the Archive button to move the messages to the Outlook Archive folder. Outlook creates this Archive folder automatically. Additionally, an AutoArchive feature can be activated using the button in the Properties group on the Folder tab.

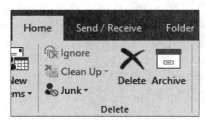

Outlook automatically created archive folders for all of the folders Ann created. The new Archive button is now available on the Home tab.

DEVELOP YOUR SKILLS OU2-D17

Saved messages often fill up active folders. In this exercise, you will move messages that you want to retain to the Archive folder.

 You can complete this exercise "live" or via the online WebSim.

1. Follow the step for your situation:
   - If using the WebSim: In your web browser, go to **http://labyrinthelab.com/2016/websim/OU2D17**.
   - If using Outlook "live": Continue with step 2.

2. Choose **File→Tools→Set Archive Folder**.

3. Click **OK** in the Archive window to select the default Archive folder.

4. Click the **Back** ⊕ button to leave Backstage view and return to your Outlook program.

5. If necessary, select the **Inbox** in the Folder pane.

6. Select the message from **Mary McKay**.

7. Click the **Archive** button in the Delete group on the Home tab.

Self-Assessment

Check your knowledge of this chapter's key concepts and skills by completing the Self-Assessment. The answers to these questions can be found at the back of this book.

1. Multiple signatures can be stored in Outlook.   *True   False*

2. When all recipients are in the Bcc box, each one sees only their own address.   *True   False*

3. Outlook can check for new messages at regular intervals automatically.   *True   False*

4. Outlook's spelling and grammar checker works to check only email messages.   *True   False*

5. You can send a message to only one recipient at a time.   *True   False*

6. If you send a message that has a file attached, the recipient cannot save the attachment to their own computer.   *True   False*

7. Quick Steps help by automating repetitive tasks.   *True   False*

8. Message list commands allow you to reply to and forward messages.   *True   False*

9. When you forward a message, Outlook automatically places the email address in the To field.   *True   False*

10. You can reply only to the original sender of a message.   *True   False*

11. How does Outlook handle new email accounts?
    A. Outlook creates the email account.
    B. Outlook supplies you with an email account.
    C. Outlook does not provide email as an option.
    D. Outlook provides you with access to your email account.

12. Which of the following is NOT a netiquette rule?
    A. Don't type in all capital letters.
    B. Do summarize your message in the subject.
    C. Don't use Arial as the font in email messages.
    D. Do use correct capitalization and punctuation.

13. How do you move a file into a folder?
    A. Choose Home→Move→Move and then choose the desired folder.
    B. Drag the message from one folder and drop it onto another folder.
    C. Either A or B
    D. Neither A nor B

14. What Outlook feature would you use to have all messages that meet certain criteria automatically moved into a specific folder?
    A. Rules
    B. Quick Step
    C. Sorter
    D. All of these options

3

Working with People

In this chapter, you will manage Outlook's People element, the electronic equivalent of a Rolodex® card file that used to be found on every desk. Outlook provides you with an address book in which to store your contacts. After you create them, you can always go back and edit or even delete contacts. Storing contacts in the Contacts list makes addressing messages much simpler than typing the addresses each time. And, the Contacts list can be sorted in numerous ways. You can search for and choose one or more recipients from the Contacts list to go into the header section of a message. In this chapter, you will also learn how to save time addressing messages to the same group of people over and over again by creating contact groups.

LEARNING OBJECTIVES

- Explore the People views
- Work with contacts
- Use contact groups
- Use the People pane

CHAPTER TIMING

- Concepts/Develop Your Skills: 1 hr 30 mins
- Self-Assessment: 15 mins
- Total: 1 hr 45 mins

PROJECT: WORKING WITH PEOPLE

Ann Hitchcock feels pretty good now about using Outlook for email, so she is ready to learn how to work with the People element of Outlook. She will learn how to enter contacts in Outlook, send messages to contacts, create groups of contacts, manage contacts, and work with the People pane.

Managing People in Outlook

Outlook offers several ways to display your contacts, or the people with whom you communicate. Don't be confused by the terminology here: Outlook calls the element where you store your contacts "people." The terms "contacts" and "people" are used somewhat interchangeably, so don't get caught off-guard.

You can save all contacts in the default Contacts folder, or you can create separate folders in which to store related contacts (such as work, school, and so forth). You can maintain varied amounts of information about different contacts in Outlook's Contacts list. For example, you may keep only Aunt Helen's email address, while, for a business client, you might want to store the company name, address, phone numbers, and email address. Contacts can be edited or deleted at any time in the People element. You can delete a contact as you delete any other item: Select it and tap Delete .

The Contacts List

There are five standard ways to view your contacts: People, Business Card, Card, Phone, and List. You can also create your own view. Which view you choose is a personal preference. The view options are found in the Current View group on the Home and View tabs when the People element is selected. As your list of contacts grows, you can scroll through the list or use the Search Contacts box to find a particular contact. You will learn more about finding contacts later in this chapter.

By default there are five standard views available in the People element of Outlook.

Peek-a-Booing with People

One feature in Outlook allows you to "peek" at your list of favorite people when you are in other elements of Outlook.

When you peek at People in Outlook, you can choose to communicate with any of your favorite contacts; exactly how you can communicate is based on the information you have entered for the person. This feature also allows you to quickly view contact information while active in other elements of Outlook, such as email addresses. When you view a peek, you can choose to dock it on the right side of your window, thereby adding it to your workspace. You will learn how to mark people as your favorites later in this chapter.

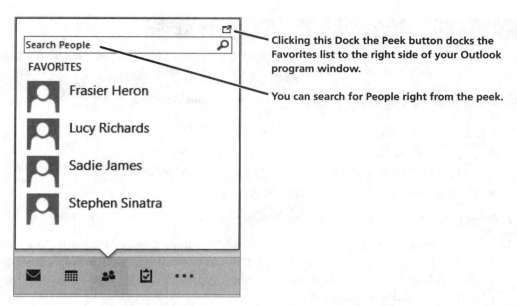

Clicking this Dock the Peek button docks the Favorites list to the right side of your Outlook program window.

You can search for People right from the peek.

When you move your mouse pointer over People on the Navigation bar, you can "peek" at your Favorites contacts.

People Toolbar

When you hold your mouse pointer over a name in Outlook, a toolbar appears. This toolbar enables you to quickly chat, call, schedule a meeting, or send an email to the person shown in your Favorites list here. Use the icons along the bottom of the toolbar to perform the action.

Click this icon to quickly send an email to Sadie.

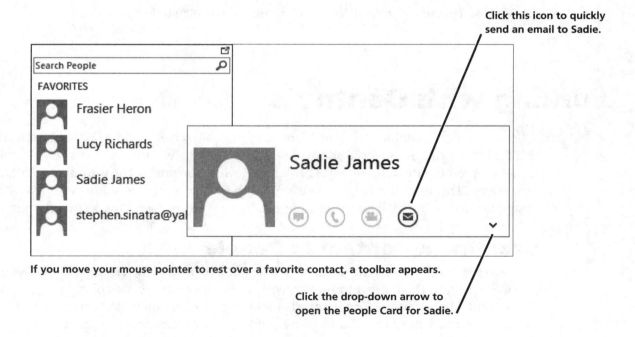

If you move your mouse pointer to rest over a favorite contact, a toolbar appears.

Click the drop-down arrow to open the People Card for Sadie.

Sometimes you need quick access to a phone number, address, or other contact information. In this exercise, you will use the peek feature to review contact information without leaving the message list.

 You can complete this exercise "live" or via the online WebSim.

1. Follow the step for your situation:
   - If using the WebSim: In your web browser, go to **http://labyrinthelab.com/2016/websim/OU3D1**.
   - If using Outlook "live": Continue with step 2.

2. Hover your mouse pointer over the People link in the lower-left part of the window.

3. Move your mouse pointer up the peek and hover it over *Sadie James* until the toolbar appears. If you aren't using the WebSim, hover your mouse pointer over any contact available. If no contacts are available, return to this exercise after assigning contacts to your Favorites (in the next exercise).

4. Click the **Send Email Message** button on the Sadie James toolbar.

5. Close the Message window, choosing to not save changes.

6. Click the **People** link in the Navigation bar to view the People element.

7. Choose **Home→Current View→Business Contact** to change the view.

8. Choose **Home→Current View→Phone** to change the view again.

9. Choose **Home→Current View→People** to return to People view.

Working with Contacts

When you create a contact, Outlook stores it in the Contacts folder of your Outlook data file. You will find it to be a time-saver to address your messages by selecting your contacts from People rather than typing them manually. The default format for storing the information is Last Name, First Name. This format is helpful because you then have an option to sort your list by either first or last name. You will learn more about sorting your contacts later in this chapter.

Creating a Contact in People

You can create a contact in the Contacts window and store as much information as you want about the person. The more information you put in, the more you will be able to see when you "peek" and when you view your contacts in the People element, which can be quite helpful. For example, you may need to call someone but don't know the number. If you had entered the phone number in People, you could view it right there in front of you.

The Social Network connector no longer connects to Facebook, LinkedIn, or other networks because the interfaces could not be maintained. The add-in for Social Network 2016 may be installed, but it is not active. One thing to keep in mind is that people can be added only individually. While you may wish to add a bunch of contacts all at once, importing a contacts file is the only way to do so.

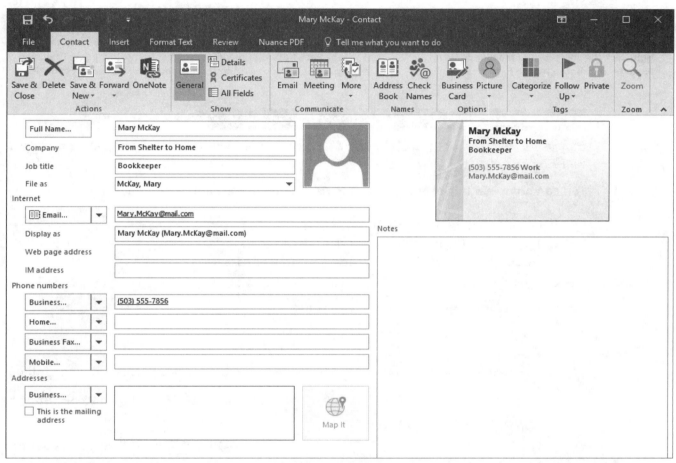

Note the fields available for you to populate when you create a new contact. You can choose the level of detail that you include in a contact record.

Turning a Person Included on an Incoming Message into a Contact

Another method of adding a contact is to right-click the email address of someone in the header on an incoming message and choose Add to Outlook Contacts. After you add it, a contact window opens automatically, giving you the opportunity to enter additional information.

Making a Contact a Favorite

To turn a contact into a favorite so you can view it on the People peek, you simply right-click it and choose Add to Favorites from the options menu. To remove a contact, you must click the Dock the Peek button in the upper-right corner of the peek. Then, you can right-click on a contact and choose Remove from Favorites.

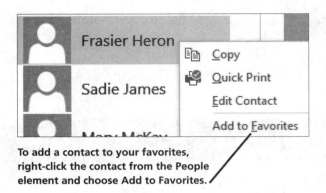

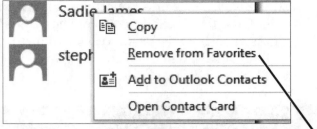

To add a contact to your favorites, right-click the contact from the People element and choose Add to Favorites.

To remove a contact from your favorites, you must click the Dock the Peek button in the upper-right corner of the peek. Then, you can right-click on a contact and choose Remove from Favorites.

DEVELOP YOUR SKILLS OU3-D2

Outlook's address book is just a click away. In this exercise, you will add a new contact to Outlook and to your Favorites.

 You can complete this exercise "live" or via the online WebSim.

1. Follow the step for your situation:
   - If using the WebSim: In your web browser, go to **http://labyrinthelab.com/2016/websim/OU3D2**.
   - If using Outlook "live": Continue with step 2.

2. Choose **Home→New Items→Contact** 📇.

3. Follow these steps to create a new contact:

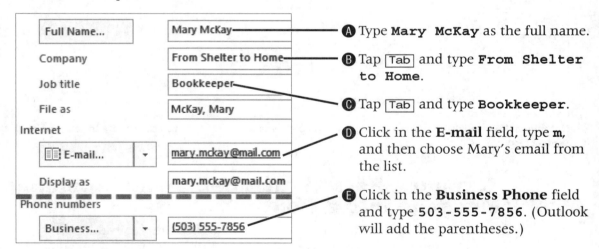

A Type **Mary McKay** as the full name.

B Tap Tab and type **From Shelter to Home**.

C Tap Tab and type **Bookkeeper**.

D Click in the **E-mail** field, type **m**, and then choose Mary's email from the list.

E Click in the **Business Phone** field and type **503-555-7856**. (Outlook will add the parentheses.)

4. Choose **Contact→Actions→Save & Close** 💾.

5. Click the **Mail** ✉ link on the Navigation bar.

6. Click **Inbox** in the Favorites list and then click the email from **Stephen Sinatra**.

7. Follow these steps to set up Stephen as a contact:

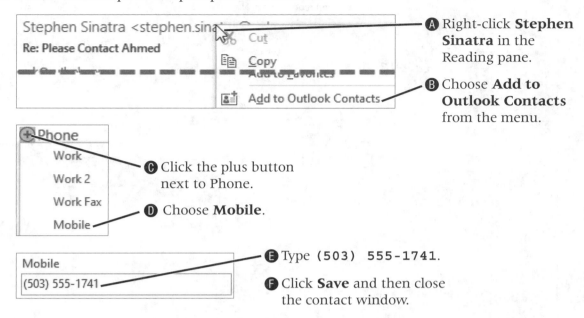

Ⓐ Right-click **Stephen Sinatra** in the Reading pane.

Ⓑ Choose **Add to Outlook Contacts** from the menu.

Ⓒ Click the plus button next to Phone.

Ⓓ Choose **Mobile**.

Ⓔ Type **(503) 555-1741**.

Ⓕ Click **Save** and then close the contact window.

8. Click the **People** 🔗 link in the **Navigation bar**.

9. Right-click **Frasier Heron** or another contact and then close the contact window and choose **Add to Favorites**.

Editing Contacts

To edit information, you must first find the desired contact and open the associated window. You can either scroll to find the contact or perform a search. When you peek at the People element, a Search People box appears at the top of the peek. If you are in the People element, you will see a Search Contacts box at the top of the list of contacts. As you begin to type in either of these boxes, the Contacts list filters contacts to display the names that contain those letters.

Another tool to aid you in locating a contact if you are in People, Business Card, or Card view is to click one of the letters along the left side of the Contact list to move to contacts that start with that letter.

Viewing People Cards

The People Card helps you to keep track of all your contact information in one easy location and can be accessed from a variety of places throughout Outlook.

You can access a People Card by double-clicking a contact in People view or by clicking the drop-down arrow at the bottom-right corner of a contact toolbar. When you open a card from a contact toolbar, you have an option to "pin" it so it does not go away when you move on to another area of Outlook. If a People Card is opened from People view, it is opened in editing mode, and there is no pin icon. If you make a change and click Save or click Cancel, you will see the pin icon and can then pin the People Card.

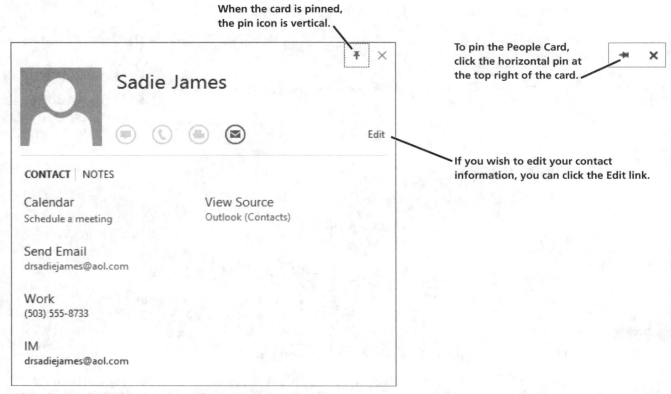

When the card is pinned, the pin icon is vertical.

Sadie James

Edit

To pin the People Card, click the horizontal pin at the top right of the card.

If you wish to edit your contact information, you can click the Edit link.

CONTACT | NOTES

Calendar
Schedule a meeting

View Source
Outlook (Contacts)

Send Email
drsadiejames@aol.com

Work
(503) 555-8733

IM
drsadiejames@aol.com

When the People Card is pinned, it will not "go away" when you move away from it in Outlook, and you can view it alongside or on top of other windows.

DEVELOP YOUR SKILLS OU3-D3

Sometimes you need to modify or add additional contact information. In this exercise, you will edit a People Card so it stores more detailed information.

 You can complete this exercise "live" or via the online WebSim.

1. Follow the step for your situation:
   - If using the WebSim: In your web browser, go to
     `http://labyrinthelab.com/2016/websim/OU3D3`.
   - If using Outlook "live": Continue with step 2.

2. Double-click **Stephen Sinatra** to open his People Card in edit mode.

3. Follow these steps to edit the contact:

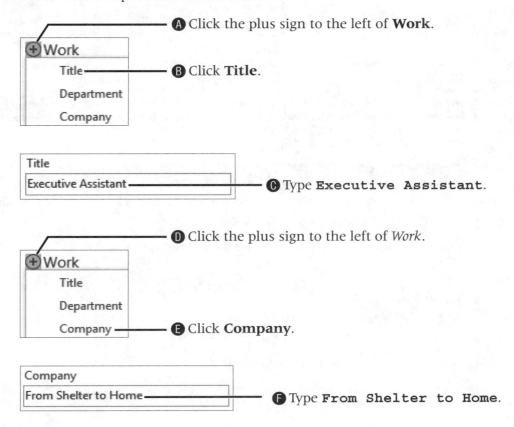

Ⓐ Click the plus sign to the left of **Work**.

Ⓑ Click **Title**.

Ⓒ Type **Executive Assistant**.

Ⓓ Click the plus sign to the left of *Work*.

Ⓔ Click **Company**.

Ⓕ Type **From Shelter to Home**.

4. Click the **Save** button.

5. Click the **pin** at the top left of the People Card window.

6. Click the **Close** button to close the window.

Sorting the Contacts List

By default, the Contacts list is sorted alphabetically by last name; however, you may wish to have it sorted differently. For example, if you deal with a variety of companies, you may wish to sort your list by company name. Or, if you have stored all your contacts by first name first, you may wish to sort by first name. When you are viewing the list in Phone or List view, you can use column headers at the top of each column for sorting. The first click on a header sorts the list in ascending order, and the second click changes the sort to descending order. When you change the sort order, it remains in that order until you change it again—even if you close and reopen Outlook. You can also change the order in which the columns appear and the width of the columns. While we don't cover it in this book, be aware that you can also choose which columns to display in the Manage All Views window.

🗋	🔖	FULL NAME	COMPANY	FILE AS ▲	BUSINESS PHONE	MOBILE PHONE	E-MAIL
		Click here to add a new ...					
👤		Frasier Heron		Heron, Frasier		(503) 555-7989	frasier.heron@yahoo.com
👤		Sadie James		James, Sadie	(503) 555-8733		drsadiejames@aol.com
👤		Mary McKay	From Shelter to ...	McKay, Mary	(503) 555-7856		mary.mckay@mail.com
👤		Stephen Sinatra	From Shelter to ...	Sinatra, Stephen		(503) 555-1741	stephen.sinatra@yahoo.com

Here, columns have been rearranged so those that Ann uses most are to the left. Note the triangle to the right of File As, which indicates that the list is sorted alphabetically by this column. If the triangle were pointing down, the list would be sorted in reverse alphabetical order.

DEVELOP YOUR SKILLS OU3-D4

Outlook allows you to sort your Contacts based on a large number of criteria. In this exercise, you choose the order in which the columns of data appear.

 You can complete this exercise "live" or via the online WebSim.

1. Follow the step for your situation:
   - If using the WebSim: In your web browser, go to **http://labyrinthelab.com/2016/websim/OU3D4**.
   - If using Outlook "live": Continue with step 2.

2. Choose **Home→Current View→Phone** 📞.

3. Follow these steps to move a column header and resize a column:

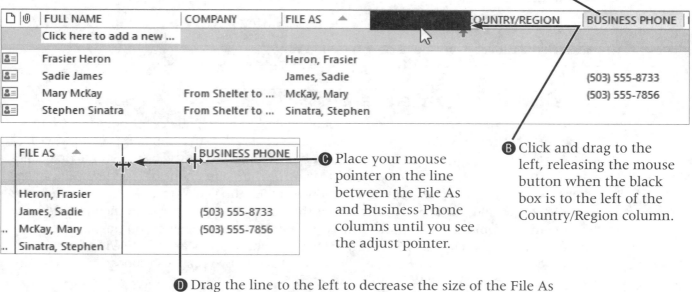

Ⓐ Place your mouse pointer over the **Business Phone** heading.

Ⓑ Click and drag to the left, releasing the mouse button when the black box is to the left of the Country/Region column.

Ⓒ Place your mouse pointer on the line between the File As and Business Phone columns until you see the adjust pointer.

Ⓓ Drag the line to the left to decrease the size of the File As column to be just large enough to fit the widest entry.

4. Click the **Full Name** column header to sort by that column. Click it again to reverse the order of the sort.

Sending Messages to Contacts

When you have contacts entered in the People element, addressing email messages is easy. When you type an email address, there is always the possibility of typing it incorrectly. In addition, as your list of contacts grows, remembering all of them becomes more difficult. After you open a new message window, you can click the To, Cc, or Bcc button to display a list of your contacts. In addition, if you begin typing a contact in the To, Cc, or Bcc field, you can choose to have it fill in for you. If you do not want recipients to see other recipient names, address the message in the Bcc box rather than the To box.

The way in which you go about sending an email from the Contacts list depends on which view is displayed. In People view, you click the Email button below the contact name in the Reading pane. In all other views, you select a contact and then choose the Email command from the Ribbon.

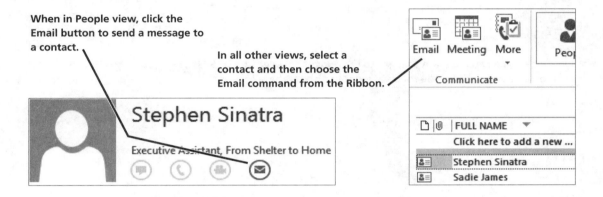

When in People view, click the Email button to send a message to a contact.

In all other views, select a contact and then choose the Email command from the Ribbon.

DEVELOP YOUR SKILLS OU3-D5

Once you have saved a person's contact information, Outlook offers shortcuts for working with that person. In this exercise, you will see how easy it is to send messages to a contact on file.

 You can complete this exercise "live" or via the online WebSim.

1. Follow the step for your situation:
   - If using the WebSim: In your web browser, go to
     `http://labyrinthelab.com/2016/websim/OU3D5`.
   - If using Outlook "live": Continue with step 2.

2. Follow these steps to send an email to Stephen from Phone view:

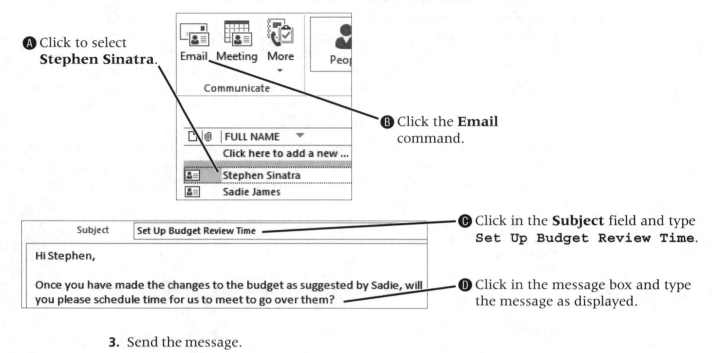

A Click to select **Stephen Sinatra**.

B Click the **Email** command.

C Click in the **Subject** field and type `Set Up Budget Review Time`.

D Click in the message box and type the message as displayed.

3. Send the message.

Working with Contact Groups

A quick way to send messages to the same group of people is to create a contact group, formerly called a distribution list. This feature can definitely save you time if you find yourself sending messages to the same group, such as a project team. When you create a group, its name appears alphabetically in the address book. When you want to send a message to the group, you address the message by using the group name, either selecting it from the list or typing it in the To box. The contacts you place in a group will still appear individually in the address book, so you can continue sending them individual messages, and they can be members of multiple groups.

Creating Contact Groups

You start creating a group by choosing the command from the Home tab in the New group. There are two options: using the New Contact Group button and choosing Contact Group from the New Items list. Both commands open a blank Contact Group window in which you give your group a name and begin adding members. You can also remove someone from a group. For example, if you create a contact group for your team and someone leaves, you can remove that person and add a replacement.

One thing for you to be aware of is that contact groups are made up of only the contacts you have listed in the People element. So, if you wish to add a new member to a contact group, you must either first add that person as a contact or add the person as a contact while creating the group. Contact groups cannot be created in Outlook with POP3 accounts such as Outlook.com and Gmail. However, you can place copies of all of your contacts in your Outlook data file and then create the groups; they just won't be available to you if you are accessing your email online. If you are working on an Exchange server, you are able to create contact groups.

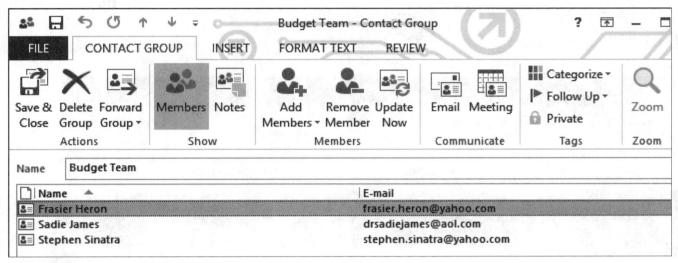

You can add contacts as members of a contact group.

DEVELOP YOUR SKILLS OU3-D6

Using groups makes it easy to communicate with a number of people. In this exercise, you will create a contact group that will allow you to send messages to many people at one time.

You can complete this exercise "live" or via the online WebSim. If working "live," create three sample contacts or use existing ones.

1. Follow the step for your situation:
   - If using the WebSim: In your web browser, go to
     `http://labyrinthelab.com/2016/websim/OU3D6`.
   - If using Outlook "live": Continue with step 2.

2. Choose **Home→New→New Contact Group** .

3. Follow these steps to create the new group:

Ⓐ Type **Budget Team** as the name.

Ⓑ Click **Add Members**.

Ⓒ Click **From Outlook Contacts**.

Ⓓ Double-click **Frasier Heron**.

Ⓔ Click **Sadie James**. Then hold down `Ctrl` and click **Stephen Sinatra**.

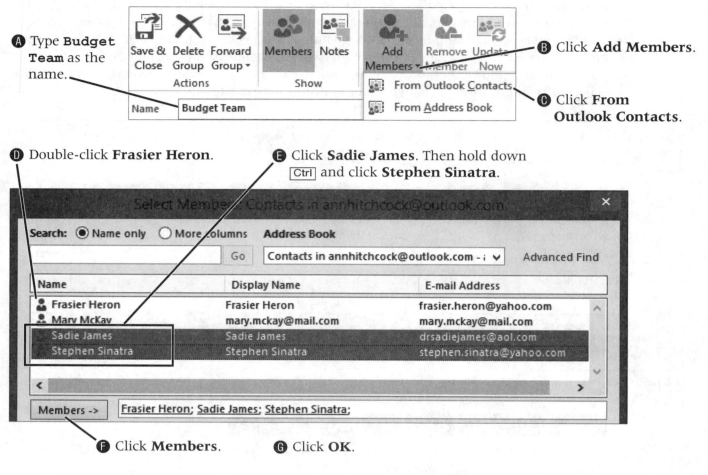

Ⓕ Click **Members**.

Ⓖ Click **OK**.

4. Choose **Contact Group→Actions→Save & Close** 🖼.

Sending Messages to Groups

When you create a contact group, its name appears in the list of contacts in alphabetical order. A contact group is denoted in the People view by an icon with multiple people on it.

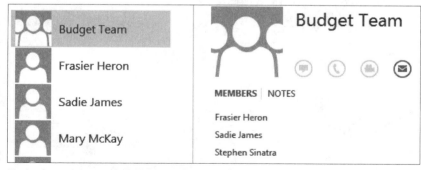

Notice how a contact group appears in People view.

To send a message to everyone in a contact group while in a new message window, you enter the group name where you normally enter a contact's name. Another easy method is to click on the Mail icon in the People pane when you have the group name highlighted in the list. This will open a new message window with the group name already in the To field.

DEVELOP YOUR SKILLS OU3-D7

Let's communicate! In this exercise, you will create a new message and send it to a group.

 You can complete this exercise "live" or via the online WebSim.

1. Follow the step for your situation:
   - If using the WebSim: In your web browser, go to
     http://labyrinthelab.com/2016/websim/OU3D7.
   - If using Outlook "live": Continue with step 2.
2. Click the **Mail** ✉ link on the Navigation bar.
3. Choose **Home→New→New Email** ⬚.
4. Follow these steps to create a message for the budget team:

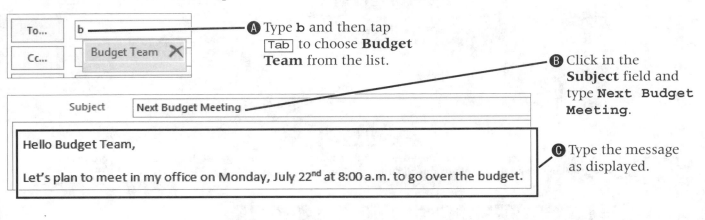

Ⓐ Type **b** and then tap Tab to choose **Budget Team** from the list.

Ⓑ Click in the **Subject** field and type **Next Budget Meeting**.

Ⓒ Type the message as displayed.

5. Send the message.

Revising a Contact Group

You can remove one member by using the Delete key or the Remove Member command in the Members group. Delete an entire group by using the Delete Group command in the Actions group on the Ribbon. When you remove a member or delete a group, you cannot undo the action. When you delete a member from a group, the contact is not deleted from your address book. However, when you edit the information of someone in the group, the address book information is automatically updated. Make sure to choose Remove Member rather than Delete Group from the Ribbon when removing a person from a contact group, or you will have to recreate the contact group from scratch. (I speak from experience on this one!)

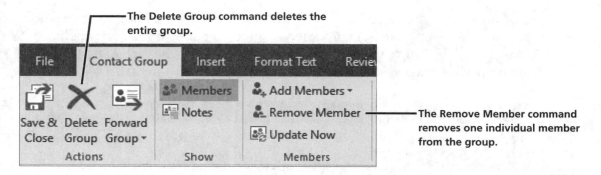

The Delete Group command deletes the entire group.

The Remove Member command removes one individual member from the group.

You can also add members to a contact group at any time by opening the group and choosing to Add Members in the same way you did when you first created the group.

One nice feature of Outlook is the drag-and-drop capability. When a contact group is created, you can drag it into an email message and send it to other Outlook users for them to add to their People element. Or you can click on the Forward Group button in the Actions group and Outlook will create an email message with the details of your group members attached.

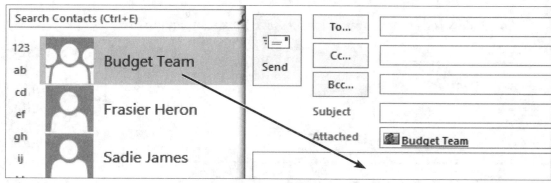

If you drag a contact group into the message field of an open email message, Outlook will add the group as an attachment and the recipients can add it to their own Contacts lists.

DEVELOP YOUR SKILLS OU3-D8

Group memberships frequently change. In this exercise, you will add a new member, for whom you don't have a saved contact, to an existing contact group.

You can complete this exercise "live" or via the online WebSim.

1. Follow the step for your situation:
    - If using the WebSim: In your web browser, go to `http://labyrinthelab.com/2016/websim/OU3D8`.
    - If using Outlook "live": Continue with step 2.
2. Click the **People** link in the Navigation bar.
3. Double-click the **Budget Team** contact group.

4. Follow these steps to add a new group member who is not yet a contact:

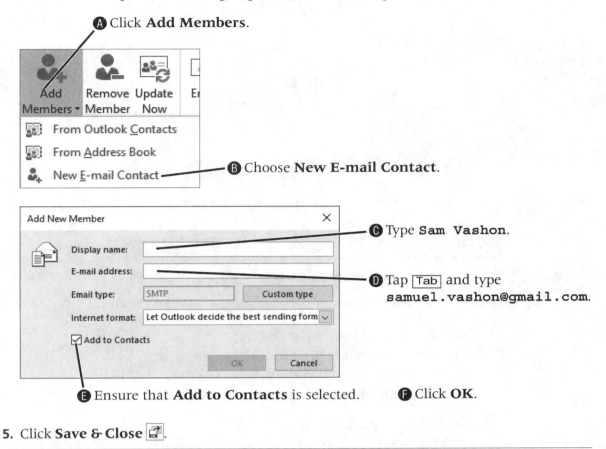

Ⓐ Click **Add Members**.

Ⓑ Choose **New E-mail Contact**.

Ⓒ Type `Sam Vashon`.

Ⓓ Tap `Tab` and type `samuel.vashon@gmail.com`.

Ⓔ Ensure that **Add to Contacts** is selected.

Ⓕ Click **OK**.

5. Click **Save & Close** 🗗.

Staying Connected with People

Outlook makes it easy to stay connected with people, not just via email, but also by tracking files and meetings and other actions in Outlook.

The People Pane

The People pane keeps track of all Outlook actions—emails, attachments, meetings, etc.—that you have with your contacts. When you are in the Mail element, the People pane can be displayed below the Reading pane or as part of the To-Do bar along the right side of the program window.

The People pane can be maximized so you can see a list of communications with a contact when you click an item, such as an email or meeting. When you activate the People pane and click an item, two icons appear on the right of the pane: One is always your icon, and the other is for the selected contact. When the pane is open, four tabs along the left side filter the items to show Mail, Attachments, Meetings, and All (this allows you to view all of the previous four options in one location).

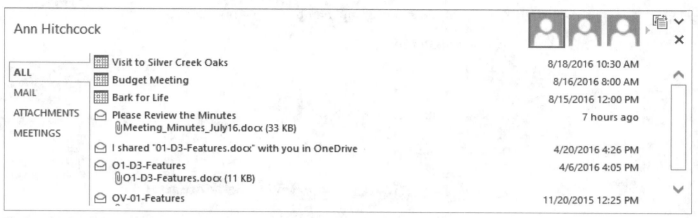

Ann Hitchcock

ALL		
	🗓 Visit to Silver Creek Oaks	8/18/2016 10:30 AM
MAIL	🗓 Budget Meeting	8/16/2016 8:00 AM
ATTACHMENTS	🗓 Bark for Life	8/15/2016 12:00 PM
MEETINGS	✉ Please Review the Minutes 📎Meeting_Minutes_July16.docx (33 KB)	7 hours ago
	✉ I shared "01-D3-Features.docx" with you in OneDrive	4/20/2016 4:26 PM
	✉ O1-D3-Features 📎O1-D3-Features.docx (11 KB)	4/6/2016 4:05 PM
	✉ OV-01-Features	11/20/2015 12:25 PM

The People pane helps you keep track of emails, files, and meetings for your contacts.

DEVELOP YOUR SKILLS OU3-D9

In this exercise, you will use the People pane as a quick way to email a contact.

 You can complete this exercise "live" or via the online WebSim.

1. Follow the step for your situation:
   - If using the WebSim: In your web browser, go to
     `http://labyrinthelab.com/2016/websim/OU3D9`.
   - If using Outlook "live": Continue with step 2.
2. Click the **Mail** ✉ link on the Navigation bar.
3. Click to select the email from Ann Hitchcock.
4. Click the expand button on the People pane.

5. Hover over the contact icons on the upper-right side of the People pane.

6. Follow these steps to send an email to Stephen Sinatra from the People pane:

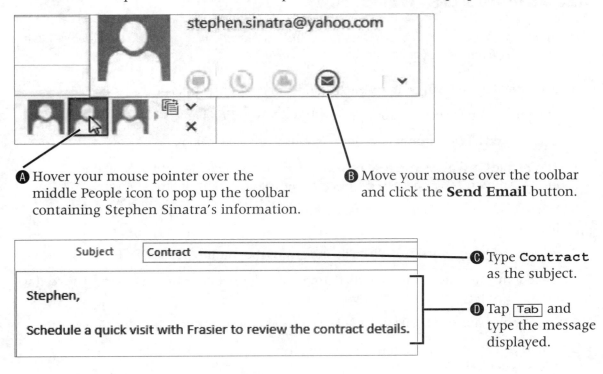

Ⓐ Hover your mouse pointer over the middle People icon to pop up the toolbar containing Stephen Sinatra's information.

Ⓑ Move your mouse over the toolbar and click the **Send Email** button.

Ⓒ Type **Contract** as the subject.

Ⓓ Tap Tab and type the message displayed.

7. Send the message.

Self-Assessment

Check your knowledge of this chapter's key concepts and skills by completing the Self-Assessment. The answers to these questions can be found at the back of this book.

1. Every field must be filled in for each contact in the Contacts list.   *True   False*

2. You can search for People from a peek off the Navigation bar.   *True   False*

3. You can add a large number of contacts at one time in Outlook.   *True   False*

4. The People Card helps you to keep track of all your contact information in one location, and it can be accessed from a variety of places throughout Outlook.   *True   False*

5. When you put a contact in a contact group, the name disappears from the complete list of contacts.   *True   False*

6. You can sort the Contacts list by clicking any of the column headers in Phone or List view.   *True   False*

7. Once someone is added to a contact group, they cannot be removed from it. The contact group must be deleted or recreated.   *True   False*

8. The People pane can keep track of your contacts' social network profiles.   *True   False*

9. When you delete a member from a group, the contact is also deleted from your address book.   *True   False*

10. To delete someone from a contact group, select the name from the opened list and tap `Delete`.   *True   False*

11. Which of the following is NOT a view available in the People Home tab, Current View group?
    A. Business cards
    B. Peek
    C. Phone
    D. People

12. What does the People toolbar associated with a contact NOT enable you to do?
    A. Quickly chat
    B. Schedule a meeting
    C. Send an email
    D. Add a new contact

13. What happens when you type a contact group name in the To box of a message?
    A. Each group member's name appears separately in the To box.
    B. The message is sent to each group member.
    C. Both A and B
    D. None of these options

14. What happens when you edit the information of someone in a contact group?
    A. The information is updated in the contact group only.
    B. You cannot edit the information of a contact in a contact group.
    C. The information in the complete address book is updated automatically.
    D. All information is deleted.

4

Working with the Calendar

In this chapter, you will learn how to use several Calendar features. Calendars are used to schedule times for meetings and appointments and to keep an eye on the weather where these meetings may occur. Depending on your needs, you can look at your calendar in different views—for example, Day, Week, or Month. You can also schedule appointments that happen on a regular basis (recurring appointments). In addition, you will learn about reminders, which are set to notify you of upcoming events. Finally, in this chapter, you will learn how to share your calendar while keeping certain items private only to you.

LEARNING OBJECTIVES

- Create and edit appointments and meetings
- Set recurring appointments
- Use calendar views
- Share your calendar
- Print a calendar

CHAPTER TIMING

- Concepts/Develop Your Skills: 2 hrs 15 mins
- Self-Assessment: 15 mins
- Total: 2 hrs 30 mins

PROJECT: WORKING WITH CALENDARS

Now that Ann Hitchcock has learned all about emailing and working with contacts in Outlook, she is ready to discover how it will help her manage her time wisely. She knows that organization is extremely important in her job: where to be at what time, whom she's meeting, for what purpose she's meeting, and so forth. Outlook's Calendar feature is the perfect place for her to keep organized. When Ann or her assistant set up appointments, reminders can also be set to pop up. When Ann starts out in the morning, she will display her calendar to see what's in store for her that day. If she needs to make appointments for later in the week, she can view her schedule for the entire week so she doesn't set conflicting appointments. Ann also wants to have a hard copy of her calendar to carry with her, and she wants to share her calendar with her assistant. She can do both with Outlook, plus she can still keep certain items on her calendar private.

Exploring the Calendar

The calendar displays your schedule in several views: Day, Work Week, Week, Month, and Schedule. The type of schedule you maintain will determine which view works best for you. For example, you can use the Work Week view if you need visible details about each business-related appointment this week, or you can use the Month view if you need to see only what dates do not currently have anything scheduled. Day, Work Week, and Week views also can display your daily tasks at the bottom of the calendar, if you select that option.

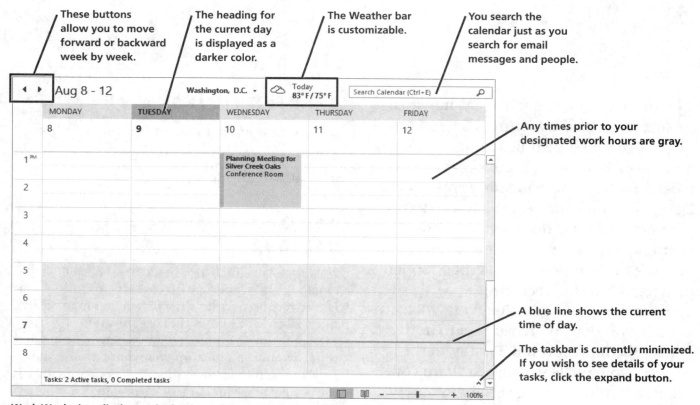

These buttons allow you to move forward or backward week by week.

The heading for the current day is displayed as a darker color.

The Weather bar is customizable.

You search the calendar just as you search for email messages and people.

Any times prior to your designated work hours are gray.

A blue line shows the current time of day.

The taskbar is currently minimized. If you wish to see details of your tasks, click the expand button.

Work Week view displays only the days of the week that you designate as your workdays.

Peeking into Your Calendar and Appointments

Just as you can "peek" at People in Outlook, you can also do the same for your Calendar. The calendar peek view shows calendar items only for the day that you have selected, so if you wish to see more items, you will need to single-click to select a different day. If you double-click, you will cause the calendar to display the day on which you clicked. In the same way, when you place your mouse pointer over an appointment, a peek at additional details about it will appear.

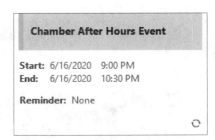

There are two calendar "peeks." One can be accessed regardless of the element you are in and shows information for a single day. The other is accessed when you are viewing your calendar and gives details about an individual appointment or meeting.

Day View

Day view displays all events on the calendar for the chosen day. The scroll bars are used to navigate the times of the day. You can change the beginning and end default time options. The Forward and Back arrow buttons display the next or previous day's calendar. You will learn about changing options later in this chapter. Day view also displays daily tasks at the bottom of the calendar, if you select this option.

When you are viewing your calendar, the Folder pane displays the current and next month.

Week View and Work Week View

Week and Work Week views are perfect when you want to check whether you have any time for an appointment in the current week. Work Week view displays only the days in your work week, which you can set if they are not Monday–Friday. Both views are similar in layout, and you can choose to display your tasks at the bottom of each of these calendars just as you can in Day view.

Month View

The Month view displays the entire month of events. Month view is handy when you want a quick look at what dates already have something scheduled and what dates you are free. You have three options of how much detail to display: Low hides all appointments, Medium displays a horizontal line in a date when something is scheduled, and High displays the appointment titles. It is also easy to copy an appointment from one day to another in Month view.

◄ ►	August 2016		☁☀ Today 87°F/76°F		Search Calendar (Ctrl+E) 🔍	
SUNDAY	MONDAY	TUESDAY	WEDNESDAY	THURSDAY	FRIDAY	SATURDAY
Jul 31	**Aug 1**	2	3	4	5	6
7	8	**9**	10 1:00pm Planning Meeting for Silver Creek Oaks; Confer...	11	12	13
14	15 12:00pm Bark for Life; Minto Brown Park	16 8:00am Budget Meeting	17	18 10:30am Visit to Silver Creek Oaks	19	20
21	22	23	24	25	26	27
28	29	30	31	**Sep 1**	2	3

Notice that in Month view, there is no taskbar, and the current day is displayed in blue.

Schedule View

Schedule view displays your daily calendar from left to right. This option may be helpful if you are viewing multiple calendars and trying to choose a time to schedule a meeting for multiple people.

DEVELOP YOUR SKILLS OU4-D1

Once your schedule is saved, you can focus on your schedule for the day, the week, or the month. In this exercise, you will explore the different options available for viewing your scheduled appointments.

 You can complete this exercise "live" or via the online WebSim.

1. Follow the step for your situation:
   - If using the WebSim: In your web browser, go to **http://labyrinthelab.com/2016/websim/OU4D1**.
   - If using Outlook "live": Continue with step 2.

2. Move your mouse pointer over the Calendar 🗓 link on the Navigation bar and then double-click on the day one week from today.

3. Click the **Calendar** 🗓 link in the Navigation bar.

4. Choose **Home→Arrange→Day** 🖼 to change the view.

5. Choose **Home→Arrange→Schedule View** 🖼 to change the view again.

6. Choose **Home→Arrange→Month** 🖼 to go to Month view.

Changing Calendar Options

Certain options for calendars can be changed via Backstage view. For example, you can change the reminder increments from the default of fifteen minutes. One of the more common options to change is the daily work times, as gone are the days of everyone working the same shift of Monday through Friday, 8:00 AM to 5:00 PM.

Adding Holidays to a Calendar

Outlook makes it easy to view holidays on your calendar to make sure you don't schedule anything that would conflict with a holiday that you or your associates may have off. If you don't want the holidays to appear on your own calendar, you can choose to display a separate holiday calendar side by side with your calendar instead.

The Weather Bar

You can view the weather in your location or any other city right from the Weather bar on your Outlook calendar.

The Weather bar allows you to align your schedule to weather forecasts, as certain weather conditions could affect your plans. You can add up to five cities to the bar, and switching from one to another is easy. It is also easy to remove a city from the bar if you hit the five-city limit so that you can add a new one if your travels take you elsewhere.

You can click the drop-down arrow next to the currently displayed city to add a city to the Weather bar.

DEVELOP YOUR SKILLS OU4-D2

Outlook provides many ways to customize your work schedule and calendar. In this exercise, you will set calendar options for your work schedule and add holidays for the United States.

You can complete this exercise "live" or via the online WebSim.

1. Follow the step for your situation:
   - If using the WebSim: In your web browser, go to `http://labyrinthelab.com/2016/websim/OU4D2`.
   - If using Outlook "live": Continue with step 2.

2. Choose **File→Options**.

3. Follow these steps to change options and add holidays to your calendar:

Ⓐ Click the **Calendar** tab.

Ⓑ Click the drop-down arrow and choose **7:30 AM**.

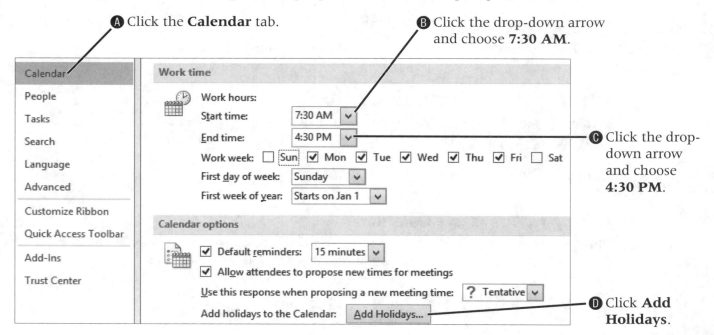

Ⓒ Click the drop-down arrow and choose **4:30 PM**.

Ⓓ Click **Add Holidays**.

4. Ensure that **United States** is selected in the Add Holidays to Calendar window and then click **OK**.

5. Click **OK** to acknowledge the addition of holidays to your calendar.

6. Click **OK** in the Outlook Options window.

Working with Appointments and Meetings

You create appointments for whenever you need time blocked out of your day. For example, you may have a doctor's appointment, have a meeting with a client, or need scheduled time to work on a task that you create. You must open an appointment window to edit information in it (such as the duration), to set a reminder, to add extra notes, and so on. You can also change an appointment time by clicking and dragging it on the calendar. You use the same appointment window to set up a meeting. The difference between a meeting and an appointment is that you can invite people to attend a meeting, whereas an appointment affects only your schedule.

Scheduling an Appointment

When you click the Calendar link on the Navigation bar, the calendar opens in the last view that you had displayed. After the calendar opens, you can double-click at the desired starting time of your appointment, or on the day you wish to schedule an appointment. After you have created an appointment, the calendar displays its title, and the shaded area indicates the duration. When you have an all-day or multiday event, you can mark it as such, and it will be displayed as a banner across the top of the day(s) that it spans.

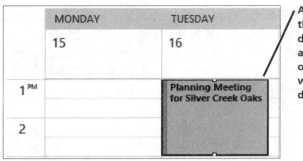

An appointment that is not a full day or more appears shaded on the calendar with the title displayed.

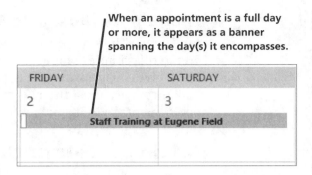

When an appointment is a full day or more, it appears as a banner spanning the day(s) it encompasses.

DEVELOP YOUR SKILLS OU4-D3

Appointments allow you to set aside scheduled time for your activities. In this exercise, you will insert a new scheduled appointment into your calendar.

You can complete this exercise "live" or via the online WebSim.

1. Follow the step for your situation:
   - If using the WebSim: In your web browser, go to `http://labyrinthelab.com/2016/websim/OU4D3`.
   - If using Outlook "live": Continue with step 2.

2. Choose **Home→New→New Appointment** 📅.

3. Follow these steps to create a new appointment:

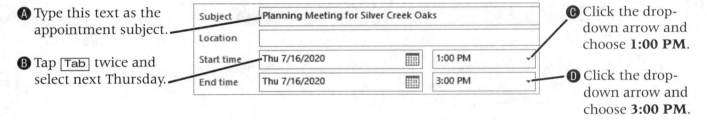

A Type this text as the appointment subject.

B Tap Tab twice and select next Thursday.

C Click the drop-down arrow and choose **1:00 PM**.

D Click the drop-down arrow and choose **3:00 PM**.

4. Choose **Appointment→Actions→Save & Close** 🔲.

Editing Appointments

You can edit any section of an appointment when you open the appointment window. For example, you can change the dates and times, set a reminder, categorize it, mark it as private, or even enter special notes for yourself in OneNote.

Changing the Appointment Time or Date

Plans change and appointments get postponed all the time. When you change the time in the appointment window, it moves the appointment to the new time slot on the calendar. Or, it's very quick and easy to move an appointment by dragging it. Moving an appointment to another day in the same week is easily done in Week or Work Week view.

Using Appointments to Manage Information

Many people find that they can use their Outlook calendars to manage a lot of information. Later in this chapter, you will learn how to turn an email message into a calendar appointment. This allows you to easily refer to the topic of the meeting without having to search through email messages. In addition, you may wish to include the agendas for meetings in your appointments so that you have them at your fingertips.

Setting a Reminder

You can set reminders to pop up on your screen or mobile devices, prompting you of upcoming events. A reminder can be set from zero (0) minutes up to two weeks prior to the appointment. By default, Outlook sets every appointment you create with a fifteen-minute reminder, and you can change this default in the Outlook Options window. Setting reminders can help anyone who has too many appointments to remember.

Changing How Appointments Are Shown

Outlook allows people to view your calendar to schedule meetings. The amount of information someone can see is determined by whether you have shared your calendar with that person. Setting the Show As option lets people with whom you work know "in general" if you are available, regardless of whether you have shared your calendar with them. By default, Outlook sets each as Busy.

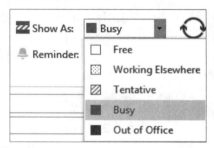

DEVELOP YOUR SKILLS OU4-D4

Things do not always go as planned. In this exercise, you will make changes to an existing appointment.

 You can complete this exercise "live" or via the online WebSim.

1. Follow the step for your situation:
   - If using the WebSim: In your web browser, go to **http://labyrinthelab.com/2016/websim/OU4D4**.
   - If using Outlook "live": Continue with step 2.

2. Double-click the **Planning Meeting for Silver Creek Oaks** appointment.

3. Click in the **Location** field and type **Conference Room**.

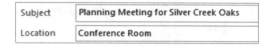

4. Follow these steps to mark the meeting as tentative and set a reminder for 30 minutes:

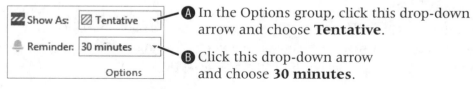

Ⓐ In the Options group, click this drop-down arrow and choose **Tentative**.

Ⓑ Click this drop-down arrow and choose **30 minutes**.

5. Click **Save & Close** 🔲.

Recurring Appointments

Recurring appointments are those that occur the same day and time each week, bimonthly, monthly, and so forth. For example, you may have a monthly Chamber meeting on Tuesdays at 5:30 PM.

Activities that happen at regular intervals (for example, weekly) can be inserted at one time in the Calendar as a series of appointments. In this exercise, you will add a recurring event to your Calendar.

 You can complete this exercise "live" or via the online WebSim.

1. Follow the step for your situation:
   - If using the WebSim: In your web browser, go to **http://labyrinthelab.com/2016/websim/OU4D5**.
   - If using Outlook "live": Continue with step 2.

2. Choose **Home→New→New Appointment** 📅.

3. Follow these steps to create the appointment:

Ⓐ Type **Chamber After Hours Event.**

Ⓑ Tap [Tab] twice and type **06/25/20.**

Ⓒ Click this drop-down arrow and choose **5:30 PM**.

Ⓓ Click this drop-down arrow and choose **7:00 PM**.

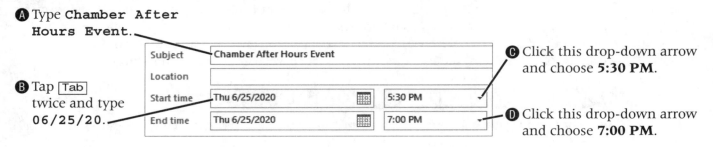

4. Follow these steps to set up the appointment to reoccur:

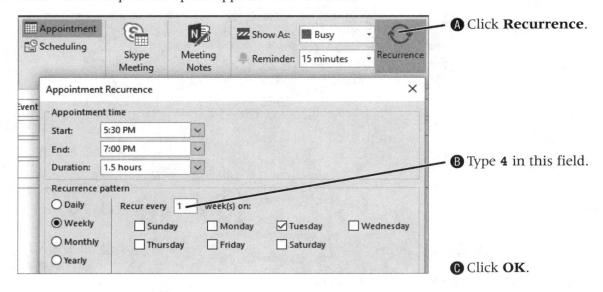

Ⓐ Click **Recurrence**.

Ⓑ Type **4** in this field.

Ⓒ Click **OK**.

5. Click **Save & Close** 💾.

Editing Recurring Appointments

You can edit just one occurrence or the entire series of a recurring appointment. When you opt to change the entire series, whatever editing you perform affects every instance of that appointment. It is important to note, however, that any exceptions you may have made for an individual occurrence will be lost when you make a change to the entire series. For example, if you change a reminder for just one occurrence but then edit the entire series to occur from weekly to monthly, the individual exception for the one reminder will remain as edited.

When you open a recurring appointment or meeting, you have the option to open just the one or the entire series.

Deleting a Recurring Appointment

When you delete a recurring appointment, you have the option of deleting only one occurrence or the entire series. For example, let's say that you set up a monthly recurring appointment for the next year but then realize you will not be available in June or December. You can delete only those two occurrences. When you want to delete the entire series, edit the entire series. When you want to delete an occurrence, edit just the one occurrence. Be careful! When you delete a recurring appointment, series, or just an occurrence, you cannot undo the action.

DEVELOP YOUR SKILLS OU4-D6

When editing a recurring appointment, you can change one occurrence or the entire series. In this exercise, you will edit a full series of recurring appointments at the same time.

 You can complete this exercise "live" or via the online WebSim.

1. Follow the step for your situation:
   - If using the WebSim: In your web browser, go to
     `http://labyrinthelab.com/2016/websim/OU4D6`.
   - If using Outlook "live": Continue with step 2.
2. Double-click the **Chamber After Hours Event** appointment.
3. Follow these steps to edit a recurring appointment:

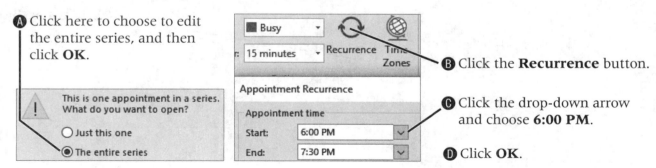

Ⓐ Click here to choose to edit the entire series, and then click **OK**.

Ⓑ Click the **Recurrence** button.

Ⓒ Click the drop-down arrow and choose **6:00 PM**.

Ⓓ Click **OK**.

4. Click **Save & Close**.

Turning an Email into an Appointment

Many times you will receive an email message that asks you for a meeting. Rather than trying to keep track of both the email message with the topic of and information for the meeting as well as the calendar item, you can use Outlook's drag-and-drop capability to turn the email into an appointment.

In this exercise, you will convert an email you have received that contains a request for a meeting into an appointment.

 You can complete this exercise "live" or via the online WebSim. If working "live," select any email message you do not need.

1. Follow the step for your situation:
   - If using the WebSim: In your web browser, go to
     http://labyrinthelab.com/2016/websim/OU4D7.
   - If using Outlook "live": Continue with step 2.

2. Click the **Mail** ✉ link on the Navigation bar.

3. Follow these steps to turn an email message into an appointment (if you are not using the WebSim, use any email message in your Inbox):

Ⓐ Drag the message from **Ann Hitchcock** down to the Calendar link and drop it.

Ⓑ Type **Conference Room** as the location.

Ⓒ Tap [Tab] and type **08/12/16**.

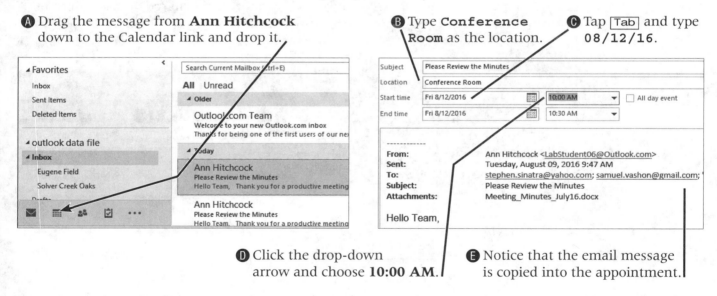

Ⓓ Click the drop-down arrow and choose **10:00 AM**.

Ⓔ Notice that the email message is copied into the appointment.

4. Save and close the appointment.

Turning an Appointment into a Meeting

When you place an appointment on your calendar, it affects only your schedule. However, you can also invite others to attend, and when you do that, the Appointment form becomes a Meeting form. At this point, not only does the name of the form change (as can be seen in the title bar of the active form) but also the Ribbon and the form itself change to provide options for scheduling your meeting and sending email invitations to each invited attendee.

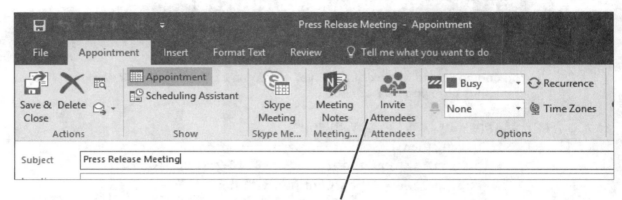

Clicking the Invite Attendees button converts the item into a meeting.

The person who creates a meeting is called the *organizer,* and the meeting is stored on that person's calendar. Only people who have editing privileges to the organizer's calendar can make changes to the scheduled meeting. This organizer role cannot be transferred to another person. If someone needs to take over the scheduled meeting, the best thing to do is to create a new meeting on the new organizer's calendar and delete the original meeting.

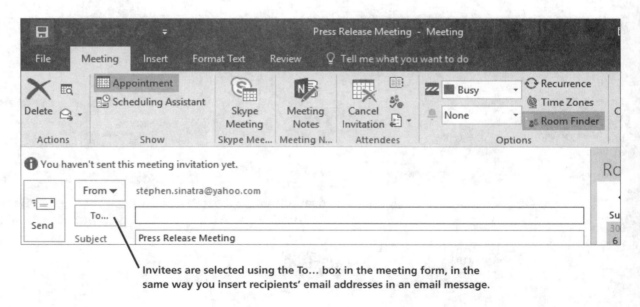

Invitees are selected using the To... box in the meeting form, in the same way you insert recipients' email addresses in an email message.

Invited attendees receive individual emails and are given the following response options on the Ribbon: Accept, Tentative, Decline, or Propose New Time. If an invitee chooses to accept or to mark as tentative, the meeting is added to their calendar and a reply can be sent to the organizer. If the invitation is declined, a reply can also be sent to the organizer. Once a meeting invitation reply is sent, the email message containing the meeting invitation disappears from the inbox.

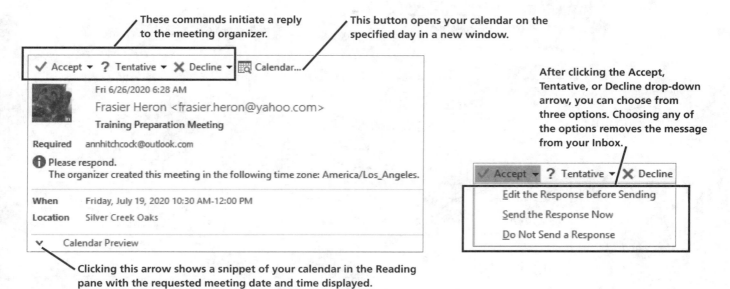

These commands initiate a reply to the meeting organizer.

This button opens your calendar on the specified day in a new window.

After clicking the Accept, Tentative, or Decline drop-down arrow, you can choose from three options. Choosing any of the options removes the message from your Inbox.

Clicking this arrow shows a snippet of your calendar in the Reading pane with the requested meeting date and time displayed.

Meetings can also be set up as recurring, and all future meetings will be hosted on the organizer's calendar. If an attendee makes a change to a meeting on a calendar, rather than waiting for the organizer to make the change, that person will not receive updates to the meeting as it is no longer "in sync" with the organizer.

DEVELOP YOUR SKILLS OU4-D8

In this exercise, you will accept an email invitation sent through Outlook that will update your calendar and invite attendees to a meeting.

 You can complete this exercise "live" or via the online WebSim.

1. Follow the step for your situation:
   - If using the WebSim: In your web browser, go to `http://labyrinthelab.com/2016/websim/OU4D8`.
   - If using Outlook "live": Continue with step 2.

2. Click on the meeting request from **Frasier Heron**. If you aren't completing this as a WebSim, click on any meeting request in your Inbox.

3. Follow these steps to accept the message:

Ⓐ Click the **Accept** drop-down arrow.

Ⓑ Choose **Edit the Response Before Sending.**

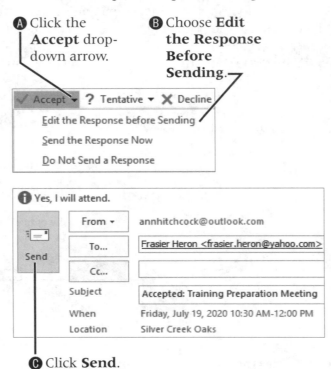

Ⓒ Click **Send**.

4. Click the **Calendar** 🗓 link in the Navigation bar.

5. Choose **Home→New→New Appointment** 🗓.

6. Choose **Appointment→Attendees→Invite Attendees** 👥.

7. Follow these steps to edit the details of the meeting:

Ⓐ Use the previously learned email list to address the message to the recipients displayed.

Ⓑ Tap Tab and type **Press Release Party**.

Ⓒ Tap Tab and type **Silver Creek Oaks**.

Ⓓ Tap Tab to move to Start Time and choose next Friday.

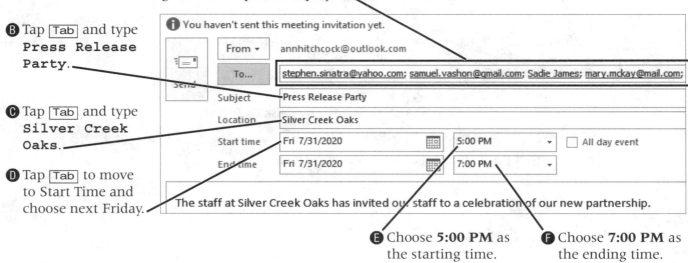

Ⓔ Choose **5:00 PM** as the starting time.

Ⓕ Choose **7:00 PM** as the ending time.

8. Send the message, choosing to save it on your own calendar if asked.

Sharing and Publishing Calendars

There are many ways to share a calendar, and this short course covers only two ways—sending a calendar via email and publishing it online. You can mark calendar items as private and then decide whether you want to share them. It's entirely up to you. The default option is to not share them. When someone receives a calendar with items marked private, all they will see on your calendar is *Private Appointment* to indicate that you are not available at that time. The sharing options will vary in the Share group on the Home tab depending on your Outlook configuration.

Notice that when you are not on a Microsoft Exchange server, the Share Calendar and Calendar Permissions options are not available on the Ribbon.

Custom Calendars

You may want a separate calendar for special circumstances. If, for example, you are working on a team project, it may be beneficial to have a special calendar to share with the project team members. You create additional calendars by using the Create New Blank Calendar command in the Manage Calendars group on the Home tab. You can also right-click the default calendar and choose New Calendar from the menu. Remember, if you share your default calendar, you can choose to keep certain items private. When you have multiple calendars, the Navigation pane displays them in a list under My Calendars.

Displaying Multiple Calendars

Multiple calendars are initially displayed side by side in the Calendar pane. When you want to check for conflicts between two calendars, overlaying them may enable you to see conflicts more easily. For example, if your project team members send you their calendars, you can overlay them to watch for conflicts and determine whether something needs to be changed. Outlook assigns calendar tabs different colors so you can easily tell them apart. When in Overlay mode, the calendar that is on the top can be edited. To change the order of calendars, click the calendar name tab at the top of the window to put the desired one on top. You can tell which items are on the bottom calendar because their titles are partially shaded (the ones on the top calendar are in bold type).

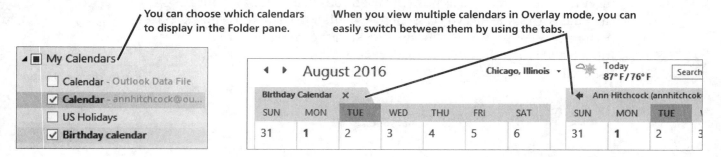

You can choose which calendars to display in the Folder pane.

When you view multiple calendars in Overlay mode, you can easily switch between them by using the tabs.

Copying Calendar Items

You can copy items from one calendar to another. The simplest way is to view the calendars side by side and drag the event over and onto the same time on the other calendar. You can also copy calendar items from one day to another on your own calendar. This is usually easiest done in Month view.

You can create calendars for different people, resources, etc. In this exercise, you will overlay different calendars to compare scheduled events.

 You can complete this exercise "live" or via the online WebSim.

1. Follow the step for your situation:
   - If using the WebSim: In your web browser, go to **http://labyrinthelab.com/2016/websim/OU4D9**.
   - If using Outlook "live": Continue with step 2. (If you do not have more than one calendar set up in Outlook, you must use the WebSim for this exercise.)

2. Click the **Birthday Calendar** checkbox in the Folder pane. If you are using your own Outlook file, you may click to the left of any of your calendars.

3. Choose **View→Arrangement→Overlay** 🗓.

Sharing Your Calendar via Email

A Calendar Snapshot is a picture of any of your calendars that you send via email to another person. Calendar Snapshots are *not* updated for the recipients when you make a change; thus, if you want your recipients to have the latest data, you will need to resend the calendar. The recipients can opt to view the calendar directly in the email message or open it as an Outlook calendar. They can then position your calendar side by side with theirs or in Overlay mode.

Marking Items as Private

Any item you have on your calendar, including appointments and meetings, can be marked as private. When you decide to share your calendar with someone, you can choose whether to share those items. An item is set as private by choosing the Private command from the Ribbon and is identified with a padlock icon at the bottom right of the event.

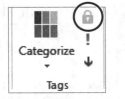

Private command button

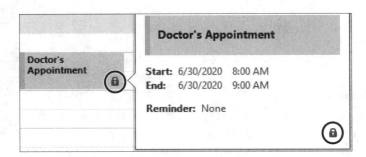

There will be a small padlock at the bottom right of the appointment as well as the "peek" when it's marked as private.

Sending Options

Use the E-mail Calendar button in the Share group to create an email message with your selected calendar attached. In the additional window, Send a Calendar via Email, you can set several options when you send a calendar to someone, such as sending the whole calendar or a specific date range. You can also specify whether you want your private items included and what layout to send it in.

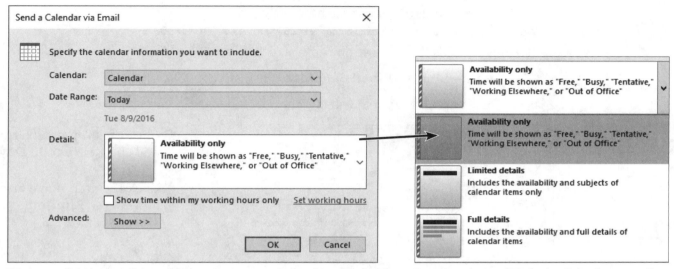

When you click the Detail drop-down arrow, you can choose from three options. Note the other options in the dialog box as well.

Publishing Your Outlook Calendar Online

If you want the person to whom you send your calendar to be able to see it, you can publish it online and then share it. This is a more dynamic way to share your calendar, and it's a good option for calendars that are tracking group projects. You will likely choose to publish your calendar to the online service that you are using for your email, such as Outlook.com.

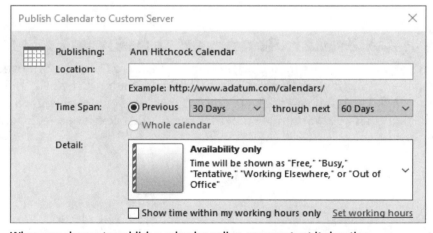

When you choose to publish a calendar online, you must set its location.

Sometimes it's helpful to share your past or future schedule with a colleague. In this exercise, you will share your calendar with someone via an email attachment.

 You can complete this exercise "live" or via the online WebSim.

1. Follow the step for your situation:
   - If using the WebSim: In your web browser, go to `http://labyrinthelab.com/2016/websim/OU4D10`.
   - If using Outlook "live": Continue with step 2.

2. Choose **Home→Share→Email Calendar** .

3. Follow these steps to share your calendar:

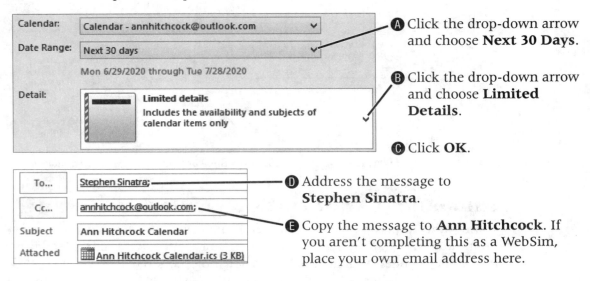

Ⓐ Click the drop-down arrow and choose **Next 30 Days**.

Ⓑ Click the drop-down arrow and choose **Limited Details**.

Ⓒ Click **OK**.

Ⓓ Address the message to **Stephen Sinatra**.

Ⓔ Copy the message to **Ann Hitchcock**. If you aren't completing this as a WebSim, place your own email address here.

4. Send the message.

Opening a Calendar Received via Email

When you receive a calendar someone sends through email, it is a Calendar Snapshot. You can read it in the Reading pane, or you can open it as an Outlook Calendar. If you open it, it will appear on the screen next to your calendar. Or, you can overlay it on top of your calendar if you wish (this can be helpful if you want to see whether any conflicts exist between your schedule and the one sent to you).

In this exercise, you will open a calendar attachment sent to you by someone else via Outlook.

 You can complete this exercise "live" or via the online WebSim.

1. Follow the step for your situation:
   - If using the WebSim: In your web browser, go to `http://labyrinthelab.com/2016/websim/OU4D11`.
   - If using Outlook "live": Continue with step 2.
2. Click the **Mail** 📧 link on the Navigation bar.
3. Click the email with the subject of **Ann Hitchcock Calendar**.
4. Double-click to open and view the calendar attachment next to your current calendar.
5. Click **Yes** in the confirmation window to open this Internet calendar.

Printing Calendars

Calendars have many options for printing. For example, you can print a Day, Week, or Month view. You can preview the calendar first in Backstage view to be sure it is the view you want to print. You can even print a blank calendar, which can be handy when you are just sitting down to think about next month's activities. To print a blank calendar, create a new calendar in a folder and print it. The following figure illustrates various print options in the Print dialog box.

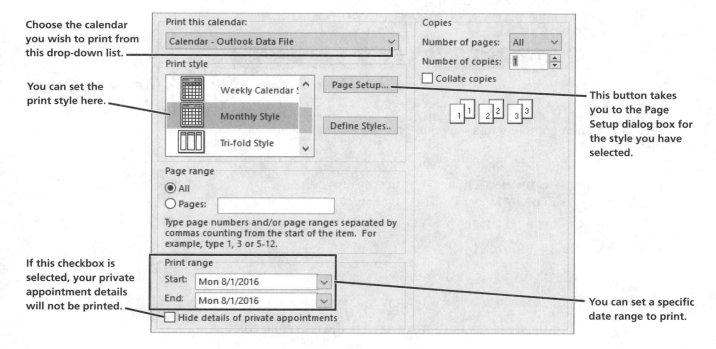

Choose the calendar you wish to print from this drop-down list.

You can set the print style here.

This button takes you to the Page Setup dialog box for the style you have selected.

If this checkbox is selected, your private appointment details will not be printed.

You can set a specific date range to print.

Page Setup

Further options are available in the Page Setup dialog box found within the Print dialog box. For example, you can set options to print the Week style in columns top to bottom or left to right, print only workdays, and add a header or footer.

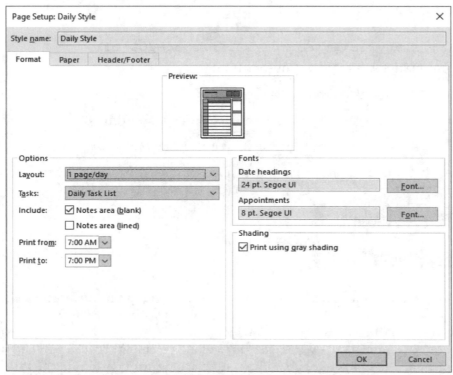

When the Daily Style is selected in Backstage view or the Print dialog box, the Page Setup dialog box will display options specific to that style.

DEVELOP YOUR SKILLS OU4-D12

Some companies still love to work on paper. In this exercise, you will print a hard copy of your calendar from Outlook.

 You can complete this exercise "live" or via the online WebSim.

1. Follow the step for your situation:
   - If using the WebSim: In your web browser, go to `http://labyrinthelab.com/2016/websim/OU4D12`.
   - If using Outlook "live": Continue with step 2.
2. Choose **File→Print**.
3. Click **Daily Style** as the setting.
4. Click the **Print Options** button and review the various settings.
5. Click the **Preview** button to return to the previous screen.
6. Click the **Back** button to return the main Outlook window.

Self-Assessment

Check your knowledge of this chapter's key concepts and skills by completing the Self-Assessment. The answers to these questions can be found at the back of this book.

1. You can undo the deletion of an occurrence of a recurring appointment.   *True   False*

2. An appointment is a time period you block off on your calendar.   *True   False*

3. You can create an appointment only by opening an appointment window.   *True   False*

4. You cannot change the start date or time for an appointment.   *True   False*

5. Your daily tasks appear at the bottom of the calendar only when it is displayed in Month view.   *True   False*

6. Recurring appointments can only be set to occur the same day and time for each week.   *True   False*

7. The Work Week view always displays the weekends.   *True   False*

8. Any item you have on your calendar can be marked as private.   *True   False*

9. A calendar sent via email is a copy of the calendar at that time; that is, it cannot be updated as your calendar changes.   *True   False*

10. When a meeting sent through Outlook is accepted, it disappears from the email folder.   *True   False*

11. How can you read a calendar that someone sends you via email?
    A. In the Reading pane
    B. Open it as an Outlook calendar
    C. Both A and B
    D. None of the above

12. When you invite others to an appointment, what is the event called?
    A. A conference
    B. A meeting
    C. A gathering
    D. A convention

13. What icon is used to indicate that an item on your calendar is private?
    A. A small padlock
    B. A circle with a slash through it
    C. A closed eye
    D. The letter P with a circle around it

14. In Outlook, what do you call appointments that occur the same day and time each week, bimonthly, monthly, and so forth?
    A. Repeating appointments
    B. Recurring appointments
    C. Periodic appointments
    D. Frequent appointments

5 Working with Notes, Tasks, and Integration

In this chapter, you will use notes, tasks, the To-Do bar, and the Folder list to integrate Outlook with other Office applications. You can also use categories to link similar information in Outlook. All Office applications integrate well together, and Outlook is no different. You will export Outlook data to Excel and use it for a Word mail merge, as well as attach a file to an appointment. Nowadays many people depend on mobile devices to keep them connected. The information that you store and work with in Outlook can be accessed on these devices. This chapter will look briefly at how this integration works.

LEARNING OBJECTIVES

- Work with notes
- Create and edit tasks
- Assign and accept/decline tasks
- Understand the Folder list and To-Do bar
- Integrate Outlook with Word and Excel
- Access Outlook information on a mobile device

CHAPTER TIMING

- Concepts/Develop Your Skills: 1 hr 15 mins
- Self-Assessment: 15 mins
- Total: 1 hr 30 mins

PROJECT: CREATING NOTES AND TASKS

Ann Hitchcock is now comfortable with the main elements of Outlook and wishes to learn more about how it can help her with her work. She has heard that she can use notes to keep track of random chunks of information that she currently keeps on sticky notes and that tasks will help her from not having to write new to-do lists each day. She also would like to see how Outlook is organized overall, and will assign categories to more easily manage information across all Outlook elements. Ann plans to learn more about Word and Excel and wants to see how Outlook works with these programs. Finally, Ann just got a new mobile device and would like to know how she can make sure that it works seamlessly with Outlook.

Working with Notes

Notes are used to record miscellaneous information you would like to save for future reference. For example, you may want to save a list of all the usernames and passwords you use, quick reminders, or, in Ann's case, maybe a little "cheat sheet" of the current status of outstanding grants. In addition to viewing your notes in Notes view, you can put them on your Desktop and view them after you minimize Outlook. You may not see a link to Notes displayed on the Navigation bar, but you can still access it by clicking the three dots to open a menu.

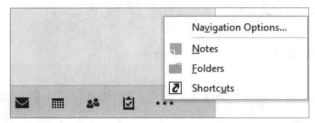

The Notes element can be accessed by clicking the three dots on the Navigation bar.

Creating a Note

When you create a note, it is stored in a special Notes folder in Outlook's personal folders. A new note opens a small box that resembles a yellow sticky note, in which you type your text. You must display the Notes view to edit or delete a note. By default, a new note will be created using yellow as the color, medium as the size, and 11-point Calibri as the font. It will also show the date and time when it was modified last.

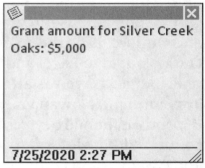

Grant amount for Silver Creek Oaks: $5,000

7/25/2020 2:27 PM

A note created with the default settings

Notes View

You can look at your notes in one of three standard views: Icon, Notes List, and Last 7 Days. You can customize the view to meet your needs and save it as a new view. You can also send a note to another person, or you can organize your notes into folders and move them to new locations.

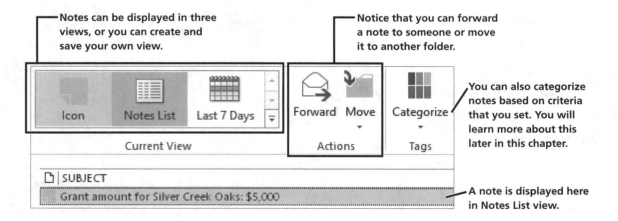

Notes can be displayed in three views, or you can create and save your own view.

Notice that you can forward a note to someone or move it to another folder.

You can also categorize notes based on criteria that you set. You will learn more about this later in this chapter.

A note is displayed here in Notes List view.

Copying a Note onto the Desktop

A convenient place to display a note is on your computer's Desktop. The note is always accessible. Double-click it to open the Outlook-independent Note window. A note window can remain open when Outlook is minimized. It is an Outlook item in the Notes folder, so you can edit or delete the note and the item is updated within Outlook. If you close Outlook, the Note windows will also close. If you close out of the note, Outlook closes the Note window, but the Note item will still be in its folder.

DEVELOP YOUR SKILLS OU5-D1

If you need to remember something, throw away the scraps of paper and try a note. In this exercise, you will create a new note and change your view.

1. Click the three dots on the Navigation bar and then choose **Notes**.

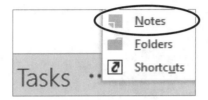

2. Choose **Home→New→New Note**.

3. Type `Grant amount for Silver Creek Oaks: $5,000`.

4. Choose **Home→Current View→Icon**.

Working with Tasks

Tasks appear in your To-Do list and contain due dates. You can set options such as a reminder, notes, or the task status. You can assign a task to others and, likewise, others can assign tasks to you. When you receive a task, you can accept or decline it. Flagged emails will also appear as tasks on your To-Do list.

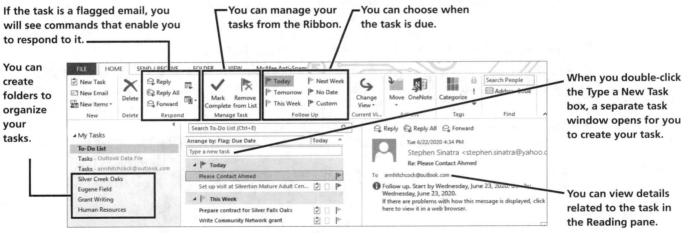

The task window with the Home tab displayed details some of the options available for a task.

Navigating Tasks

The list of task views is displayed by choosing the Tasks link from the Navigation bar. There are several ways to view your task list; the default is by To-Do list with the Reading pane situated on the right. You can also see current tasks due at the bottom of the calendar in Day, Week, or Work Week view.

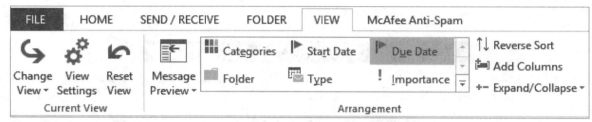

The View tab provides commands that help you set up how your tasks are displayed.

Taking a Peek at Tasks

The final "peek" we cover in this book is a peek at your tasks. You can access a peek by hovering your mouse over the Tasks link in the Navigation bar.

Creating a Task

Tasks are usually created in task view. When you create the task, it appears in the To-Do list and the To-Do bar when you have those panes displayed. You can also create a pre-populated task by dragging an Outlook item to Tasks on the Navigation bar, as you did when you created an appointment from an email message.

The To-Do Bar

You can choose to view the To-Do bar in any of the Outlook elements, and you can also customize what you want it to display—Calendar, People, and/or Tasks. The command is accessed on the View tab in the Layout group of the Ribbon, regardless of the element in which you are currently working.

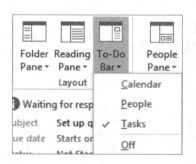

Scheduling Calendar Time to Work on a Task

When you create a task, you can drag it onto your calendar to schedule yourself time to work on it. While not mandatory, doing this simple extra step helps keep you from booking yourself too heavily with appointments. Until it is marked as complete, the task follows you on the calendar from day to day as a constant reminder. On the date you mark the task complete, it remains on that day of the calendar as a visual reminder of when you accomplished it.

In this exercise, you will create a new task that will appear in your To-Do list and To-Do bar when they are displayed.

 You can complete this exercise "live" or via the online WebSim.

1. Follow the step for your situation:
   - If using the WebSim: In your web browser, go to `http://labyrinthelab.com/2016/websim/OU5D2`.
   - If using Outlook "live": Continue with step 2.

2. Click the **Tasks** ☑ link on the Navigation bar.

3. Choose **Home→New→New Task** ☑.

4. Follow these steps to set up a new tasks:

Ⓐ Type this text as the task's subject.   Ⓑ Click this calendar button and select today's date.   Ⓒ Click this calendar button and select the date two weeks from today.

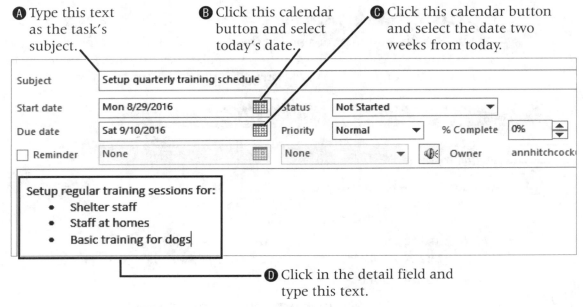

Ⓓ Click in the detail field and type this text.

5. Click **Save & Close** 🗗.

Editing Tasks

You can edit a task in task view, or directly from the To-Do bar. When you click a task on the To-Do bar from any element of Outlook, you will see a contextual tab appear on the Ribbon. If you double-click the task, it opens in its own window. Some edits you can make include changing the start and due dates, setting a date and time to be reminded, tracking the status, adding a category, and adding notes to the task. Tasks disappear from the lists when they are deleted or marked complete; however, a completed task still appears in task view with a line through the text. While there are many methods in which to mark a task as complete, the quickest way is to simply click the flag icon next to the task.

When you select a task on the To-Do bar, you will see a contextual tab appear.

Setting a Reminder

When you set a reminder for a task, a small window appears on the screen at the specified date and time. Just as you may hit snooze on your alarm clock, you can request to be reminded again in five minutes or up to two weeks, at which time the Reminder window reopens.

DEVELOP YOUR SKILLS OU5-D3

In the business world, it's important to stay on top of deadlines. In this exercise, you will edit a task by adding a reminder.

 You can complete this exercise "live" or via the online WebSim.

1. Follow the step for your situation:
   - If using the WebSim: In your web browser, go to **http://labyrinthelab.com/2016/websim/OU5D3**.
   - If using Outlook "live": Continue with step 2.

2. Double-click the **Set up quarterly training schedule** task.

3. Follow these steps to set up a reminder for the task:

Ⓐ Click here to set a reminder.

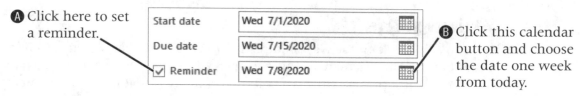

Ⓑ Click this calendar button and choose the date one week from today.

4. Click **Save & Close** 🖼.

Assigning Tasks

You can assign a task to someone or receive a task assigned to you from someone else. When you are creating a task and decide to assign it to someone, Outlook adds an address box to the task window for you to enter the recipient's address, much like when you choose to turn an appointment into a meeting. After you send the task, you no longer own it; the recipient is the new owner. When the recipient receives the task, he or she can accept or decline it. As soon as a task is accepted, it

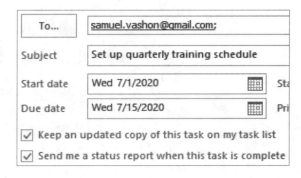

disappears from the Inbox and appears in the recipient's task list. You can also choose to keep a copy of the task in your task list and request to be notified when the task is marked complete. If you create a task for yourself and set a reminder, and then later assign it to someone else, the reminder is turned off (because you are no longer the owner).

When you choose to assign a task, the Manage Task group on the Ribbon will reflect this change.

Accepting or Declining an Assigned Task

When you assign a task, the recipient has the option of accepting or declining it. If the recipient accepts it, you will be notified via email that it was accepted (and it appears automatically in the recipient's task list). Recipients can choose to notify you upon declining the assigned task.

When you are assigned a task, you can choose whether to accept or decline it.

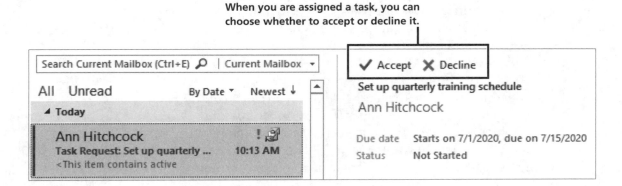

DEVELOP YOUR SKILLS OU5-D4

Do you delegate or reassign work? In this exercise, you will assign an existing task to someone else.

You can complete this exercise "live" or via the online WebSim.

1. Follow the step for your situation:
   - If using the WebSim: In your web browser, go to **http://labyrinthelab.com/2016/websim/OU5D4**.
   - If using Outlook "live": Continue with step 2.
2. Double-click the **Set up quarterly training schedule** task.
3. Choose **Task→Manage Task→Assign Task** .
4. Click in the **To** field and type **samuel.vashon@gmail.com**. If you aren't using the WebSim, please use the email address of one of your classmates.
5. Click **Save & Close** .

Working with the Folder List and Categories

The Folder list and Categories are two aspects of Outlook that pertain to all elements. The Folder list shows how all elements and folders are organized in relation to one another and is displayed in the Folder pane. Categories can be assigned to all types of items to provide color coding, similar to how you might color-code a manual filing system.

The Folder List

The folders in Outlook are arranged in a hierarchy in which the top folder is always at the Outlook data file level. If you have multiple accounts in Outlook, each one will have its own folder at this level. All of the folders related to each Outlook data file are contained inside this main one. You can add a folder directly inside the main folder, or you can create a subfolder inside another folder (for example, creating subfolders inside the Inbox to keep messages organized). Archive folders that were previously discussed are also at the Outlook Data File level. A triangle next to a folder indicates that it has subfolders. If the triangle is solid black, it means the folder is expanded and all subfolders are visible; if the triangle is just an outline, the folder is collapsed.

Renaming Folders

If you have multiple Outlook data files, you may wish to provide a descriptive name for each so that you can easily keep track of them.

▲ annhitchcock@outlook.com
  ▲ Inbox
     Eugene Field
     Silver Creek Oaks
   Drafts (This computer only)
   Sent Items
   Deleted Items 2
   Birthday calendar
   Calendar
   Contacts
   Journal (This computer only)
   Junk E-mail
   Notes (This computer only)
   Outbox
  ▷ Sync Issues (This computer only)
   Tasks 4
   US Holidays
   Search Folders
▷ Outlook Data File
▷ Archives

Moving to Another Element by Using the Folder List

Just as you use the Navigation bar to switch among Outlook elements, you can do the same with the Folder list. Click a folder representing an Outlook element (Inbox, Calendar, Contacts, or Tasks) in the Folder list, and that element will be displayed.

DEVELOP YOUR SKILLS OU5-D5

Are you tired of switching between messages, people, tasks, etc.? In this exercise, you will explore the flexibility offered by the Folder list.

1. Click the three dots on the Navigation bar and then choose **Folders**.

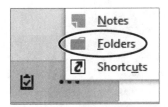

2. Click **Calendar** 📅 in the Folder list.
3. Click **Inbox** 📧 in the Folder list (below the current and next month calendars).
4. Click the **Mail** icon on the Navigation bar to return to that view.

Categories

Outlook categories allow you to color-code items in all elements based on criteria that you choose. This means that you might choose the color blue and a category name of Silver Creek Oaks to track all email messages, calendar appointments and meetings, contacts, tasks, and notes that are related to your work with that organization. Or you could organize your Outlook items by designating business as red and personal as yellow.

Once you have created and assigned categories, you can sort by them. So, if you are in People, you can choose to display all contacts that are color-coded blue and relate to the Silver Creek Oaks project. In addition, you can assign a shortcut key to categories so that assigning them is even easier.

You can set and assign categories by using the Categorize command on the Ribbon. ⎯

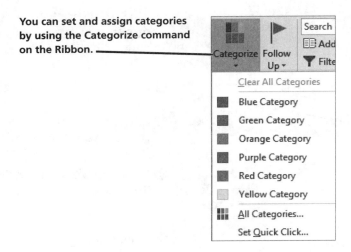

Outlook 2016 shows a new menu option at the end of the Categorize list—Set Quick Click— which opens a window to let you decide the default category. Like the Follow Up flag, with which you click and set Follow Up to Today, the Set Quick Click determines which category is automatically assigned when you click in the Category column on a message. After you pick a color with Set Quick Click, that color will display at the top of the Categorize list.

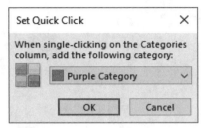

Assign a default category with the Set Quick Click window.

DEVELOP YOUR SKILLS OU5-D6

Grouping your Outlook items by category helps you organize. In this exercise, you will set and assign categories to items in Outlook.

 You can complete this exercise "live" or via the online WebSim.

1. Follow the step for your situation:
   - If using the WebSim: In your web browser, go to **http://labyrinthelab.com/2016/websim/OU5D6**.
   - If using Outlook "live": Continue with step 2.

2. Choose **Home→Tags→ Categorize ▦→All Categories**.

3. Follow these steps to set up categories:

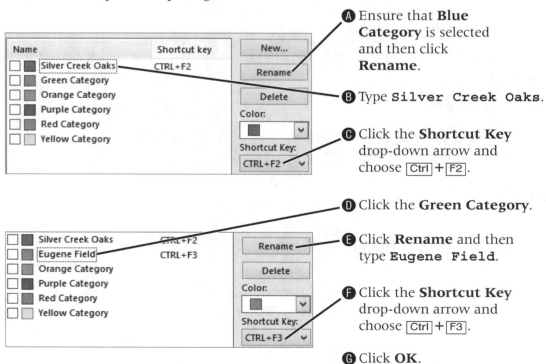

Ⓐ Ensure that **Blue Category** is selected and then click **Rename**.

Ⓑ Type **Silver Creek Oaks**.

Ⓒ Click the **Shortcut Key** drop-down arrow and choose ⎡Ctrl⎤ + ⎡F2⎤.

Ⓓ Click the **Green Category**.

Ⓔ Click **Rename** and then type **Eugene Field**.

Ⓕ Click the **Shortcut Key** drop-down arrow and choose ⎡Ctrl⎤ + ⎡F3⎤.

Ⓖ Click **OK**.

4. Follow these steps to assign a category to an email message:

Ⓐ Click to select the **Silver Creek Oaks** subfolder.

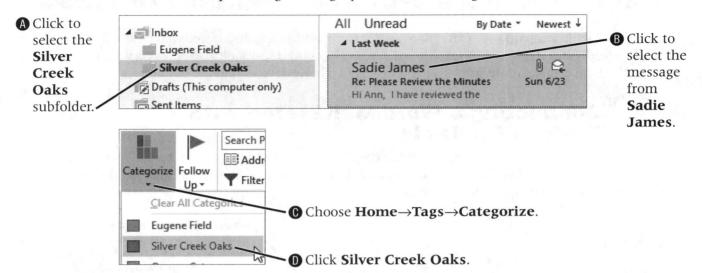

Ⓑ Click to select the message from **Sadie James**.

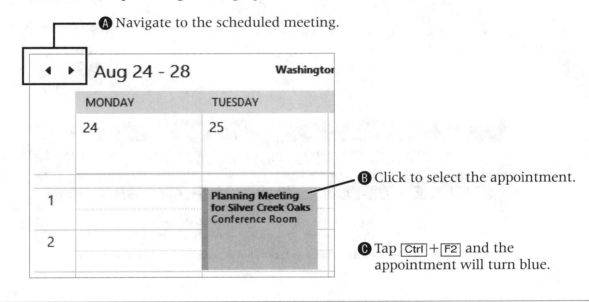

Ⓒ Choose **Home→Tags→Categorize**.

Ⓓ Click **Silver Creek Oaks**.

5. Click the **Calendar** 🔲 link in the Navigation bar.

6. Follow these steps to assign a category to a calendar item:

Ⓐ Navigate to the scheduled meeting.

Ⓑ Click to select the appointment.

Ⓒ Tap Ctrl + F2 and the appointment will turn blue.

Integrating with Word and Mobile Devices

As you wrap up your Outlook course, you no doubt have discovered that Outlook is a powerful program that can do a lot to help keep you organized. Outlook also plays very nicely with other Office applications as well as the variety of mobile devices that are out there.

Conducting a Word Mail Merge with Outlook Contacts

Outlook contacts are organized as a database, and these contacts can be exported to Excel so that you can use them for a different project, or you can access them from Word in order to conduct a mail merge with them.

When completing a mail merge in Word and you choose to Select Recipients from your Outlook Contacts, you will be able to select from which contact folder you wish to pick.

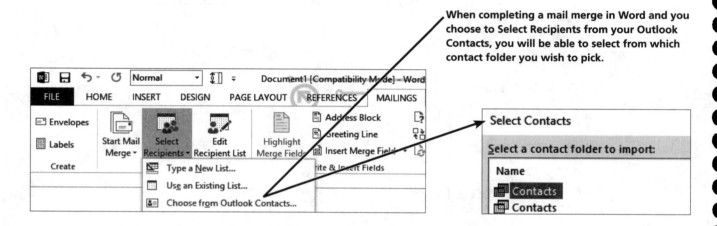

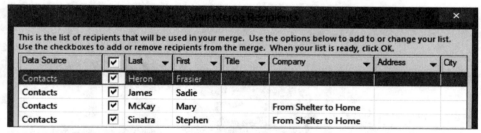

After you have selected a contact folder, you can choose whether to include all or just selected contacts.

Just as you can attach files from other Office applications to email messages, you can attach them to appointments and meetings to keep the files that you need handy. Notice that the Attach File button includes the jump list menu that is new in Outlook 2016. This provides quick access to recently opened files. You no longer have to browse to find the attachment!

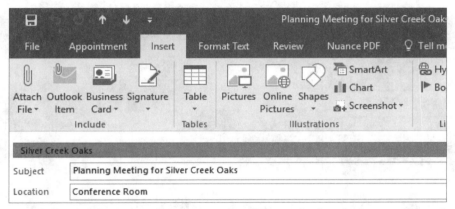

From the Insert tab, you can choose to attach a file to a calendar appointment or meeting.

Working Seamlessly with a Mobile Device

Many people have mobile devices such as smartphones and tablets for personal and professional use. The information that you access through Outlook can also be accessed on your mobile devices. Microsoft Outlook is now available for Android, iOS, and tablet devices. It can be downloaded directly into the device from the corresponding stores—Apple App Store, Google Play, Microsoft Store—as a free app. Although your email can be configured in other email apps on these devices, the Outlook app offers a familiar interface and can synch email, contacts, appointments, and tasks. Even reminders will display on your device.

For all email apps, to set up your accounts on your mobile device, you will need some data, including your email address/username and password. If it's an Exchange server, you will also need the name of the server and, possibly, the domain and knowledge of whether it uses SSL.

In the Outlook app, adding a new account uses an Auto Account setup wizard like the Outlook desktop app covered here. You may find a quicker setup and installation of your email by using the Microsoft Outlook app. Like other email apps, you can set up the Outlook app to use a variety of email accounts.

The process for adding an account in the Outlook app on a mobile device is similar to the process for the Outlook desktop app.

After your account is set up on a mobile device, you can view your email as well as reply, forward, move, and more.

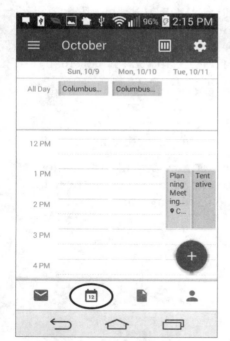

In Outlook on your mobile device, you can add, change, and delete Calendar items.

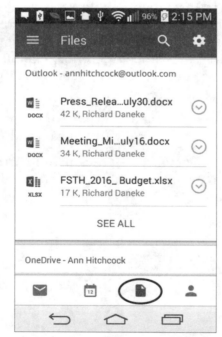

Outlook.com and Office365 accounts also let your work with cloud-based file storage.

The People pane synchronizes the details of your contacts. Add, change, or delete information and it will sync with your Outlook desktop app.

Self-Assessment

Check your knowledge of this chapter's key concepts and skills by completing the Self-Assessment. The answers to these questions can be found at the back of this book.

1. You can use Outlook contacts when conducting a mail merge in Word.   *True   False*

2. When you close Outlook, any notes on the Desktop are deleted automatically.   *True   False*

3. Categories allow you to color-code items only within the task and mail elements of Outlook.   *True   False*

4. When you assign a task to someone, you are no longer the owner of the task.   *True   False*

5. The only information you access through Outlook data that you can also access on a mobile device is your email.   *True   False*

6. Tasks can be viewed in other elements of Outlook on the To-Do bar.   *True   False*

7. Flagged emails appear as tasks on your To-Do list.   *True   False*

8. A note can have a due date and a reminder set as options.   *True   False*

9. You can accept or decline a task assigned to you by someone else.   *True   False*

10. You can create a prepopulated task by dragging an Outlook item to Tasks on the Navigation bar.   *True   False*

11. When viewing the Folder List, what is always the top folder?
    - **A.** Outlook Data File
    - **B.** Email Inbox
    - **C.** Favorites
    - **D.** Archive

12. Which of the following is NOT a view available for your notes?
    - **A.** Last 7 Days
    - **B.** Notes List
    - **C.** Icon
    - **D.** Subject

13. Which of the following can you NOT display in the To-Do bar?
    - **A.** Notes
    - **B.** Tasks
    - **C.** Calendar
    - **D.** People

14. Which aspect of Outlook pertains to all elements?
    - **A.** Folder list
    - **B.** Categories
    - **C.** Both A and B
    - **D.** None of these options

Self-Assessment Answer Key

CHAPTER 1: GETTING STARTED WITH OUTLOOK 2016

Item	Answer	Page Number
1	False	2–3
2	True	9–10
3	False	3
4	True	7
5	False	7
6	True	2
7	True	4
8	True	11
9	False	5
10	True	12
11	B	4
12	A	5
13	C	2
14	D	4

CHAPTER 2: WORKING WITH EMAIL

Item	Answer	Page Number
1	True	25
2	True	22
3	True	34
4	False	31
5	False	22
6	False	27
7	True	47
8	False	36
9	False	39
10	False	38–39
11	D	18
12	C	21
13	C	46
14	A	48

CHAPTER 3: WORKING WITH PEOPLE

Item	Answer	Page Number
1	False	60
2	True	58–59
3	False	61
4	True	63
5	False	68
6	True	65
7	False	68
8	False	61
9	False	71
10	True	71
11	B	58
12	D	59
13	B	68
14	C	71

CHAPTER 4: WORKING WITH THE CALENDAR

Item	Answer	Page Number
1	False	86
2	True	82
3	False	82
4	False	82
5	False	79
6	False	85
7	False	79
8	True	91
9	True	92
10	True	89
11	C	94
12	B	82, 88
13	A	92
14	B	85

CHAPTER 5: WORKING WITH NOTES, TASKS, AND INTEGRATION

Item	Answer	Page Number
1	True	110
2	False	101
3	False	107
4	True	105
5	False	111
6	True	102
7	True	101
8	False	100
9	True	105
10	True	102
11	A	106
12	D	100
13	A	102
14	C	106

Index

NOTES

NOTES

NOTES

NOTES

NOTES

NOTES